"THE KNEELING ANGEL"

By Niccolo dell' Arca. (Church of San Domenico, Bologna)

THE APPRECIATION OF ART

BY

EUGEN NEUHAUS

ASSOCIATE PROFESSOR OF ART IN THE UNIVERSITY OF CALIFORNIA

GINN AND COMPANY

BOSTON · NEW YORK · CHICAGO · LONDON
ATLANTA · DALLAS · COLUMBUS · SAN FRANCISCO

FEB 5 1

The Athenæum Press

GINN AND COMPANY · PRO-
PRIETORS · BOSTON · U.S.A.

TILL AMERICA HAS LEARNED TO LOVE ART, NOT AS AN AMUSEMENT, NOT AS A MERE ORNAMENT OF HER CITIES, NOT AS A SUPER-STITION OF WHAT IS *COMME IL FAUT* FOR A GREAT NATION, BUT FOR ITS HUMANIZING AND ENNOBLING ENERGY, FOR ITS POWER OF MAKING MEN BETTER BY AROUSING IN THEM A PERCEPTION OF THEIR OWN INSTINCTS FOR WHAT IS BEAUTIFUL, AND THEREFORE SACRED AND RELIGIOUS AND AN ETERNAL REBUKE OF THE BASE AND WORLDLY, SHE WILL NOT HAVE SUCCEEDED IN THAT HIGH SENSE WHICH ALONE MAKES A NATION OUT OF A PEOPLE, AND RAISES IT FROM A DEAD NAME TO A LIVING POWER.—JAMES RUSSELL LOWELL

PREFACE

Primarily this book aims to be of service to students who feel the need for a reasoned presentation of the fundamental principles that underlie the theory and the practice of all the arts. The general reader also will find here a treatment of those questions that are so constantly met with when art is the topic of discussion. It has grown out of a professional experience with large undergraduate classes of nontechnical students in the University of California, in the Extension Division of that university, and in Mills College.

Usually courses in the history of art offer to college students the means of familiarizing themselves with the achievements of art. However, the extensive field of information that has to be covered in such courses does not admit of a more than casual discussion of fundamental principles. Thoughtful teachers are not unmindful of the importance of fundamentals, particularly in our day when application of principles is often attempted without understanding. The teaching of art, not unlike that of science, must build on a solid foundation. To this end, many colleges and universities offer, in addition to courses in the history of art, courses in æsthetics. Such courses, however, excellent as they are, frequently call for extensive prerequisites in philosophy and psychology, and therefore do not meet the conditions of that large number of students who can spare only a limited time for elective work in which they are interested. All those who have had close contact with the needs of students will, I think, agree that it is a mistake to take for granted a knowledge of the fundamental principles of æsthetic appreciation.

The term "æsthetic," although a bugbear to many students, is unavoidable in a book that lays claim to be a reasoned presentation of art principles. The "æsthete," whose sincerity is often questioned, has at times cast discredit upon æsthetics and its scholarly representative, the æsthetician. The term "æsthetics," as derived from the Greek, has, however, been in common use in many languages for several hundred years and is more satisfactory than any of the cumbersome phrases— such as "the philosophy of the beautiful, "the philosophy of taste," or "the philosophy of the fine arts"—that form its equivalents. The single term has persisted largely on account of its brevity and because in its literal meaning as the Greeks used it, "fitted to be perceived," it most nearly describes the process of art enjoyment.

The æsthetician, briefly, is concerned with the examination of those psychological phenomena, the feelings, that underlie the enjoyment of beauty, and also with the critical objective examination of works of art, in an effort to discover the qualities that constitute beauty and cause pleasurable feelings. It is with this second phase of the study of æsthetics that we shall largely be concerned, in our effort to promote the critical enjoyment of art.

It will be readily admitted that an artist achieves the fullest understanding of that form of art through the medium of which he endeavors to express himself. It is not within the power of any one individual to acquire a technical mastery of all art media, and in this instance the acknowledgment must be made that the author's technical experience lies in the field of the graphic arts. It is a generally accepted fact, however, that the principles underlying all the arts are akin; and therefore this book, although it obviously offers explanation in many instances through a discussion of examples of the visually enjoyable arts, is an attempt to lay foundations for a general appreciation of art, which may be further developed according to the line of individual interest.

The writer is aware of the existence of a great number of excellent books on art,—its history, theory, and practice,— to the authors of many of which he is greatly indebted for inspiration and pleasure. He nevertheless hopes that this book may prove itself valuable within the sphere of its intended use. Many of the most important books represent the results of special researches based upon extensive experience in some art,—an experience not shared by the average person. While the tendency in some art books—although not in those excellent books that deal with design in a practical way—is to deal with art in a historical sense, stressing the *who, where,* and *when,* here we shall try to emphasize the *why* and *how.*

The author's aim in writing this book has been to treat of art as a whole, embracing, aside from æsthetic principles, its general relations to society, not in the attempt to cover the subject exhaustively, but rather in a suggestive way as an introduction to and groundwork for further studies.

In the main the subject has been developed along two avenues of approach: first, a purely æsthetic consideration of the subject,—its content and formal values; and, second, a general consideration of elements that help to influence the currents of art,—that is, the social and economic forces that are active in the domain of art.

The material covered in this book should be sufficient for a one-hour or two-hour course for one semester, as a preparation for courses in the history of art; or, where the program does not admit of this, it may be used as collateral reading. It is highly desirable that, as far as possible, local illustrations be used; only thus will art become of real meaning to the student. Teachers should make every effort to relate local material to the discussions. To an intelligent teacher mentally and æsthetically alert the problems of his own time and environment should offer a particular interest.

We may observe in this country, along with an increased interest in art, or perhaps on account of it, constantly improving opportunities for the study of art in every form. Unfortunately, ideal conditions for such study will be found only in the oldest communities, where large and splendid museums and other centers of activity have been developed. However, where such abundant opportunities for the practical study of original expressions of art do not exist, reproductions will serve the purpose. Practically all the works of art referred to in the text, when they do not appear as illustrations, are obtainable in the form of prints.

Training in the appreciation of art cannot begin too early. A systematic cultivation of the latent powers should be attempted in every division of our educational system, beginning at least in the last year of the high school.[1] Our high schools, on the whole, while they are making marked progress in the field of mechanical and vocational arts, do not yet offer much in the field of æsthetic training, and in the universities and colleges the need for æsthetic training of all students is not denied by the authorities.

The names of art institutions and individuals who kindly permitted the reproduction in this book of works of art accompany the illustrations. For the examples of artistic furniture I am indebted mainly to Vickery, Atkins and Torrey of San Francisco, and to Roberson's of London. To these and to the artists who so generously responded to my request for examples of their work I wish here to express my appreciation.

I am further indebted to my colleague Professor A. L. Kroeber, Curator of the Anthropological Museum of the University of California, for permission to photograph arrangements of Greek vases and examples of American and Asiatic art.

Mrs. Deborah Dyer Calkins, Associate in English in the Extension Division, suggested many corrections and improvements in the manuscript. The obligations that a teacher owes to his students are well known, and I cannot refrain from here thanking my students for the pleasure of many discussions which stimulated the form and selection of subject matter of this book.

EUGEN NEUHAUS

BERKELEY, CALIFORNIA

[1] The relation of art to education is discussed in the last chapter, where an attempt is made to define briefly the scope, character, and responsibility of all educational agencies that help to promote the understanding and enjoyment of art.

BIBLIOGRAPHY

ABENDSCHEIN, ALBERT. The Secret of the Old Masters. 1909.

ALLEN, GRANT. Physiological Æsthetics. 1877.

BALFOUR, HENRY. The Evolution of Decorative Art. 1893.

BELL, CLIVE. Art. 1913.

BELL, RALCY HUSTED. The Philosophy of Painting. 1916.

BOSANQUET, BERNARD. History of Æsthetics. 1904.

BROWN, G. BALDWIN. The Fine Arts. 1917.

BURGER, FRITZ. Einführung in die Moderne Kunst. 1917.

CAFFIN, CHARLES H. How to Study Pictures. 1906.

CARR, J. COMYNS. The Ideals of Painting. 1917.

CARTER, HUNTLY. The New Spirit in Drama and Art. 1913.

COX, KENYON. Artist and Public. 1914.

CRAM, RALPH ADAMS. The Ministry of Art. 1914.

CRANE, LUCY. Art and the Formation of Taste. 1885.

CRANE, WALTER. Line and Form. 1900.

DOW, ARTHUR WESLEY. Theory and Practice of Teaching Art. 1912.

EDDY, ARTHUR JEROME. Cubists, Post-impressionism. 1914.

FAURE, ÉLIE. History of Art. Translated by Walter Pach, 1909.

GORDON, KATE. Æsthetics. 1919.

GROSSE, ERNST. Die Anfänge der Kunst. 1894.

HAMERTON, PHILIP GILBERT. Thoughts about Art. 1874.

HENRI, ROBERT. The Art Spirit. 1923.

HIRN, YRJO. The Origins of Art. 1900.

LIPPS, THEODORE. Æsthetik. 1905.

LUCKIESH, MARION. The Language of Color. 1918.

MATHER, FRANK JEWETT, JR. Estimates in Art. 1916.

MEIER-GRAEFE, JULIUS. Modern Art. English translation, 1908.

MOORE, GEORGE. Modern Painting. 1898.

MOREAU-VAUTHIER, CHARLES. The Technique of Painting. 1917.

MORRIS, WILLIAM. Hopes and Fears for Art. 1882.

MÜNSTERBERG, HUGO. The Principles of Art Education. 1905.

MUTHER, RICHARD. The History of Modern Art. 1896.

NOYES, CARLETON. The Gate of Appreciation. 1907.

PARKER, DEWITT H. The Principles of Æsthetics. 1920.

PARTON, JAMES. Caricature and other Comic Art. 1878.

PHILLIPS, LISLE MARCH. Art and Environment. 1914.

POORE, HENRY RANKIN. Pictorial Composition and the Critical Judgment of Pictures. 1903.

POTTIER, EDMOND. Douris and the Painters of Greek Vases. Translated by Bettina Kahnweiler, 1916.

PUFFER, ETHEL. The Psychology of Beauty. 1905.

REINACH, SALOMON. Apollo, An Illustrated Manual of the History of Art throughout the Ages. 1904.

ROSS, DENMAN. A Theory of Pure Design. 1907.

ROSS, DENMAN. On Drawing and Painting. 1912.

ROWLAND, ELEANOR. The Significance of Art. 1913.

RUSKIN, JOHN. A Joy Forever. 1880.

RUSKIN, JOHN. Lectures on Architecture and Painting. 1854.

SANTAYANA, GEORGE. The Sense of Beauty. 1897.

STURGIS, RUSSELL. How to Judge Architecture. 1903.

TAFT, LORADO. Modern Tendencies in Sculpture. 1918.

TAINE, HIPPOLYTE ADOLPHE. The Philosophy of Art. English translation, 1867.

VAN DYKE, JOHN C. Art for Art's Sake. 1893.

VAN DYKE, JOHN C. How to Judge of a Picture. 1888.

VAN DYKE, JOHN C. The Meaning of Pictures. 1903.

VAN DYKE, JOHN C. What is Art? 1910.

VÉRON, EUGÈNE. Æsthetics. English translation, 1879.

VOGT, VAN OGDEN. Art and Religion. 1921.

WALDSTEIN, CHARLES. The Study of Art in Universities. 1896.

WOODBURY, CHARLES. Painting and the Personal Equation. 1919.

WRIGHT, WILLARD H. Modern Painting. 1915.

CONTENTS

LIST OF ILLUSTRATIONS

LIST OF ILLLUSTRATIONS

THE APPRECIATION OF ART

I

INTRODUCTION—THE ARTIST AND THE PUBLIC

Among the many problems of education none seems so fraught with difficulties as that of bringing the artist and the people together upon a common basis of mutual understanding. To allow the various products of the artist to be the exclusive and only means of communication; to depend upon them alone to produce enlightenment, without any educational preparation on the part of the public, has not been and is not, today, productive of the best results. The chasm still remains, and even becomes wider, as one experimenting school of art after another presents new problems which the layman seems unprepared to receive with interest or even with respect. Everywhere people seem to derive encouragement from the apparent contradiction involved in the variety of art to persist in their belief that all that is necessary in order to settle the question of æsthetic responsibility is to express a personal choice.

We are all acquainted with the person who admits that he knows nothing about art, but who "knows exactly what he likes." This admission may be justifiable in the person of scant educational advantages, but the person to whom modern educational opportunities are available should not find it necessary to adopt such an attitude.

As a people we of America have long been concerned with practical problems. For nearly a century our energies and talents have been applied to the sterner problems of industry, agriculture, and commerce, and the United States for many decades offered but scant promise of the unfolding of art.

I

While it is an uncontested fact that in the past the mercantile and industrial character of our American world dominated our national affairs, we have now become so prosperous that an interest in art, at least as a luxury, has become inevitable. In fact, we have in recent years not only lost our national inertia with respect to art but also developed an interest in it which is no affectation; indeed this interest has become a significant element in our affairs.

The World War, and its subsequent and inevitable disillusionments as to the permanent value of material things, have served to crystallize the idea among us that national greatness and leadership must be linked with the ideal achievements of art, and this widening of our horizon has developed an interest in all the arts and has caused a very marked increase in the number of those who are eager to approach the subject from a serious point of view. Art as a profession is no longer objected to either on practical or on social grounds; in fact, the number of young people contemplating a career in art is a very distinct indication of the change of point of view in this country.

On the other hand, we cannot entirely ignore certain factions in society which still continue inert in their attitude toward art. In the first group we still meet with the man to whom art is effeminate, perhaps even an interest of the weakling whose physical shortcomings do not permit him to take an active part in the practical constructive problems of the day. His type is fast disappearing, it is true. But we shall have to consider also types of the more confirmed objectors to art. Among these we find the puritan, who is somewhat jealous of his morals lest his human endowments may lead him to succumb to the sensuous element in art and eventually corrupt his standards. His prejudices are often merely acquired, and not so deeply rooted that they cannot be overcome.

Then there is the Philistine, who is unable to lift himself beyond the immediate realities, to whom everything is useless that cannot be applied to some immediate practical need.

Still less can we afford to overlook the proletarian, who, it must be admitted, has a real cause for his attitude. As art ceases to be a luxury, however, his objections ought gradually to disappear. His feeling toward art may well parallel the evolution of his attitude toward the automobile, which he at one time regarded as a luxury beyond his reach. During this time the plutocratic motorist in his roadside predicaments had to suffer the taunts and jeers of the mob. Then, with the introduction of the inexpensive small motor car, the man who had distributed nails upon the road as a protest against extravagance began to ride in his own automobile and to regard it as a necessity. Similarly, as fine expressions of art become so plentiful that they fall within the notice and the reach of the proletarian it is probable that he will learn to regard them as desirable and necessary.

In spite of all antagonistic elements, it is a matter of common observation that few human activities enlist so many zealous admirers as the professions that lead to the production of works of art. Many times one may hear at art exhibitions the ingenuous exclamations of enthusiastic appreciators to the effect that they would give much if only they might know how to paint a picture. This attitude we find extended in varying degrees to the other arts—literature, music, architecture, sculpture; but no art seems so generally rated as the essential medium for æsthetic satisfaction as painting. Although the ability to paint a good picture is denied to the average person, it has become a growing practice to visit galleries and museums and discuss the relative merits of works of art.

However, the people have some very positive views as to what a work of art should be, and the artist often holds with equal emphasis ideas contrary to those of the public. This condition at once places a twofold responsibility upon artists; for while working primarily to satisfy themselves and earn the respect of their profession, they must in addition please a public which is not always able to meet the artist on his own ground. Let us take some scientific profession—that of the engineer, for instance—for contrast. The engineer may usually ignore the public, and produce entirely for the satisfaction of his clients and the relatively small numbers of his fellow engineers. His standards are based upon the study of *facts*: he refuses to trust his *feelings* as to whether a bridge is safe or not, and he insists upon mathematical proof. It is different with an artist. The artist is motivated by his feelings, and he must trust that others may feel as he does. It is largely this fundamental difference between facts, on the one hand, and feelings, on the other, which makes so difficult the task of fixing a criterion in art. It is a very perplexing situation, to artist and public alike, that their judgments often differ so widely—to the artist because he cannot understand what he is inclined to call the whims of the public, and much more so to the public, because it frequently discovers that those artists on whom it sets the stamp of its approval are not those whom the profession would put on a pedestal.

But what is this public, and is it worth being taken into account by the artist? The public, in the sense in which we shall use the term, does not include the small number who have been students of art all their lives, or that small coterie equipped with the same artistic instincts as the producing artist but without a power to express their emotions through any medium. We speak of the latter as people with marked artistic perception; we speak of them as connoisseurs. They do not themselves produce, but their instinctive judgment and sympathy have made them most valuable aids and advisers of the artist. When they have been so fortunate as to possess both wealth and power, they have at times been saviors of the arts, and an artist's utopia would not be possible without them. However, they are unfortunately so few and far between that as a class they neither need nor invite any attention; they really are not the public.

The term "public," then, as here applied, has reference to that rather large, heterogeneous body of individuals who make up our general society. We have no right to underestimate the

number of those who wish to be able to respond sympathetically to the individual appeal of art in as many forms as possible. It is because they are so numerous, indeed, that it is
doubly necessary that everything should be done to help direct
their instincts into the channels which lead to real perception
and full enjoyment.

Some are firmly convinced that among the well-to-do an
understanding of artistic efforts is more widely found than
among the poor. If this be true, it is due not so much to a
keener innate instinct of artistic perception or to inherited
tendencies in the former class as it is to more frequent opportunities for study and to experience based on more intimate
acquaintance with art. On the other hand, in the case of the
rich, we cannot ignore the fact that often wealth has increased
faster than taste. The successful man is not infrequently the
man who has accumulated only wealth and power, and who
feels that with money and power nothing is unattainable. That
there are standards based upon other than monetary values
does not always occur to the "successful" man, and consequently his judgment on art is not the most dependable. The
poor, as may be observed everywhere, are not destitute of a
sense of beauty, as many think them. While they may be
compelled by force of circumstances to gratify their taste by
modest means, they offer many convincing evidences to the
observing student that they possess a love of color and of
form; and their love of music needs no comment.

The presumption, then, will not be denied that all human
beings possess an innate desire to recognize and enjoy the
beautiful, both in art and in nature, but often are unable to
expand this latent desire into a capacity for wider understanding and greater enjoyment. The view that an understanding
of art is not to be hoped for without the possession of a creative
talent unfortunately still exists in some quarters, and some
people undoubtedly deprive themselves, by reason of this idea,
of many special pleasures in life. All the arts become intelligible and enjoyable through the study of basic principles.

That training in the perception of beauty among rich and poor alike is fundamentally a problem of education becomes evident when one recognizes that discerning appreciation is the result of awakened desire, of knowledge of those principles evolved by long usage and common understanding. The public, then, particularly in a democracy, is well worth taking into account.

Fortunately all the arts are dependent for their appeal upon demonstrable qualities and laws which may be understood in a great measure by any serious-minded intelligent person, without the absolute necessity of technical experience.

It is a widely appreciated fact that many of those who have contributed conspicuously toward a more universal appreciation of many different arts belong to the literary profession. The technical devices of the literary artist permit him to discuss many other arts; for literature, so to speak, is an art within the arts. Indeed, through literature we may treat of architecture, painting, music, the drama, the dance; but it is doubtful whether any of the other arts, with the exception of the graphic arts, are capable of accurately defining the qualities of their sister arts. However, a literary artist, in considering the other arts, may allow himself to be carried away into imaginary notions that are oftentimes divergent from those of the creators of such works. Architects, sculptors, painters, and musicians alike have at times complained about what they call the literary exploitations of their efforts, and often their grievances have not been wholly unfounded. There is no doubt that those arts which are not expressed in oral or written language are at a disadvantage in expressing their ideas. And although speech is universal, the fact remains that the language of art, as it speaks to us through a statue, a painting, a piece of music, may convey a meaning which ordinary language utterly fails to express. If a new race should fall heir to the remains of our civilization, it would hardly be capable of appreciating the literature of its predecessors. Beauty, however, in every form would assert itself through innumerable agencies visually comprehensible.

The artist, not without justification, contends that the important elements in art are the qualities of formal beauty as much as subject interest. It is upon an application of these formal principles, as much as upon a knowledge of historical events, of the physical appearance of a country, of the activities of people, or of descriptive facts, that a work of art must depend for lasting merit. Without the understanding of these formal principles it must therefore remain difficult to make any progress in the acquisition of what we may term an ability to judge and enjoy the beautiful.

It is only fair that as soon as a picture is exhibited and has become common property, the artist must allow the public to make of his picture whatever it pleases. After all, the meaning of a picture to an individual is dependent on what he is able to get out of it or able to put into it.

On the other hand, if more of our artists other than writers would apply their abilities toward educating the public along formal and technical lines, in the principles of composition, color, theory, and design, they would greatly contribute toward the solution of the economic problems of artists, and the public would learn how to recognize merit in works of art.

Unless he is a man of unusual command of language, the talking artist rarely enjoys an audience. But, after all, he is a teacher in the field of art, and as necessary as the teacher in any other field; he is as useful as any person who, through educational endeavors, takes the public into the inner mysteries of his profession.

Unquestionably the greater number of artists do their work instinctively. They joyfully dispose of line and form, area, tone and color, in two or three dimensions, according to intuition, and they are rarely able to explain their reasons any further than to say that their feelings tell them theirs is the right way. The purely technical side of the artist's work naturally offers a complicated problem. By the artist himself it is often treated with unwarranted secrecy bordering on mysteriousness; but it is no more subtle than the æsthetic foundation which has been evolved from the experiences of the past and which, although it seems bewildering and baffling, is capable of ready comprehension. Our rapidly growing American interest in art is certainly deserving of the best we can offer in art education, and we cannot longer complain of lack of opportunities for study at home. But as long as the interest is focused exclusively upon the significance of subject matter (that is, the content of a work of art) and as long as little concern is manifested in abstract artistic qualities as expressed in form, it will never give to an individual anything but an unreliable and incomplete appreciation. Obviously, then, the artist himself, who knows most about his own work, must learn to recognize his responsibility in the matter of educating the public. While the creation of works of art will always remain the privilege of a few, the enjoyment of art should be increasingly cultivated by every individual.

II

THE BEGINNINGS OF ART—THE CLASSIC EXAMPLE

As far back as we can trace the history of humanity, there do we find art. The love of the beautiful has apparently always existed in man, for we find it disclosing itself in various ways as far back as the earliest periods in which any account of him can be traced. This is demonstrated by the fact that no stage of human existence has been discovered which has not left evidence of progress in the arts; indeed, this progress has grown out of the vital needs of the human race. Primitive man needed implements to insure his existence, to satisfy the demands for creature comforts; he needed them as weapons for hunting and for tilling the soil, and also as a means of storing and preparing foods. At first his devices were rudimentary, but eventually he contrived to shape them so as to distinguish them from those of other members of his tribe. In the course of time he developed that pride which led him to strive in fashioning them for what, since the dawn of human life, has been recognized as beauty. From the very earliest days, then, these objects have been improved by man in the direction not only of use but also of beauty.

The Frenchman Élie Faure[1] gallantly accords to woman the distinction of having been the first artist, his theory being that man was entirely too preoccupied with the practical requirements of life.

However this may be, it is generally accepted that the first form of art was that which developed on a utilitarian basis. Following this came attempts toward imitative representation, in which objects such as birds and animals were delineated on natural walls. Eventually, through centuries, the power of

[1] Élie Faure, History of Art.

9

communication of the æsthetic reaction of the artist developed to a point where it could be expressed by symbols, in the forms which we now recognize as the arts.

These æsthetic responses of the artist are stimulated by the various aspects of nature, which thus become interpreted in the light of his emotional experiences. From a review of the earliest development of æsthetic creation, then, it is clear that "art" is a term of extremely broad significance.

It is well known that children show the earliest mental development in the recognition of bright colors and sounds, and that they early recognize strong contrasts of every kind. If the analogy between the development of a child and that of the race at large be correct, primitive man was charmed by bright flowers and gay-plumaged birds, by clear, strong notes, and by all natural sights and sounds that were vivid and had a clearly defined sense of

ANCIENT PERUVIAN VASE
From the collection of the University of California

the value of contrast. Modern man, sophisticated though he be, is still subject to the charm of these same influences. Observe the summer camper, amusing himself by imitating the voices of birds or by scratching outlines of animals on the surface of rocks or on the sands of the beach, and you will see primitive man engaged in artistic creation.

Primitive art of this sort, then, was undoubtedly to a large extent an imitative effort; but eventually it developed beyond the stage of imitation and became sufficiently creative to develop pleasurable forms and patterns, as expressed in pottery, basketry, and metal work. At the present day the very popular craftsmanship of the Navajo and many other Indian tribes demonstrates the high standards of beauty developed on this utilitarian basis among our so-called primitive peoples.

In America we are fortunate in that the processes of primitive art may be studied so widely in the arts and crafts of the

A PERUVIAN PONCHO
American Museum of Natural History, New York

native American Indians, many of whose products are possessed of a formal beauty instantly arousing the admiration, even the envy, of the white man. The very earliest expressions of primitive art in Europe are drawings of the cave dweller incised in soft stone, mostly of animals such as the mammoth, the bison, and the reindeer. These imitative drawings are of the most realistic sort, and most astonishing in their keen understanding of form and action. Centuries after the period of the cave dweller a more advanced civilization developed the lake dwellings. In general, nothing so fascinating and realistic as the cave man's animal drawings has ever been found in the remains of these later periods, although quantities of useful implements of clay and metal have been discovered which testify to the decorative, creative sense of their producers.

INDIAN BASKETS

The one on the right is Alaskan; that on the left is from Santa Ynez; and the little one is a Ponca feather basket. (Southwest Museum, Los Angeles)

The feeling for beauty has constantly increased in variety and application of expression from the most primitive ages through the early historic art periods. Among the first of these periods, the Assyrian and the Egyptian, we find works of art indicating the remains of a great civilization. Although the evidences of artistic achievement in Assyria are relatively meager, we have in Egypt examples of magnificent architecture and sculpture, in pyramids and temples and colossal statues dating back to the very dawn of history. The evidences of the skill and taste of the Egyptian craftsman are numerous.

Doubtless the greatest period of art in Europe of which we have any extensive knowledge is that of the Greeks. Their various ways of thinking and of doing things, their whole philosophy of life, were guided by the dictates of the laws of the beautiful. Probably no nation ever felt that the true, the good, and the beautiful are one in the same simple, instinctive way that the Greeks felt it. Only under the influence of such a

COLOSSAL FIGURES, THEBES, EGYPT

thought could they produce the beautiful, as they did, simultaneously in literature, sculpture, and architecture. Their very objects of use were shaped and created with the same thought of beautiful expression as their more monumental artistic productions in sculpture and architecture. We have become so convinced of their superiority in expressing things in a beautiful way that nowadays the word "classic," derived from the standard of the Greeks, has become the highest praise we can bestow on any work of art. It is most fortunate that at so early a date in recorded history we should have been furnished with expressions of art of many kinds fit to become guiding examples for later civilization. We possess today many specimens of Greek art which are the inspiration of all

THE DOOR OF THE AGORA, ATHENS

artists of the present time and which are not likely to be surpassed or even equaled, particularly in the case of sculpture and architecture. The Greeks have given us the formula, the A B C, by which we can attempt expressions of our own civilization in artistic form. Unfortunately, however, the formula is often all that many so-called modern artists ever recognize in Greek art, and they believe that they achieve the classic quality by the meaningless use, let us say, of rows of Greek columns.

The Greeks gave us the fundamental principles of idealization, the means of expressing ordinary things in an ennobled way. The art of the Greeks was guided primarily by an understanding of the fitness of things, and will be further discussed in a later chapter. Their costumes, for instance, were both practical and beautiful, and conducive to a perfect development of their bodies. Their vases, urns, and vessels generally had proportions and shapes that fitted them equally for utilitarian and æsthetic purposes. Their architecture, domestic and monumental, never lost sight of the requirements of simplicity and fitness, and became æsthetically satisfactory through these qualities and through soundness of construction and careful workmanship.

A JAPANESE BUDDHA
From the collection of the University of California

We may, when we tire of the example of the Greeks, turn our eyes toward the Orient, where art has flourished since time immemorial. Here artistic attention to utilitarian objects is carried astonishingly far. The Chinese, while their architecture and sculpture rarely take the form of great monuments such as we find in Egypt and Greece,—except for the pagodas and some isolated animal figures of great size,—manifest a real capacity for the artistic expression of a great multitude of ordinary things. The Oriental artist (or artisan, if we must make this distinction) shows a persistent regard for fitness, and great originality in meeting constructive problems. The Orient is the inexhaustible treasure house of art. Aside from architecture and substantive sculpture, its bronze vessels, its carvings in wood, ivory, jade, and other hard and soft stones, its lacquer ware involving mysterious processes, charm even the uninitiated. Furthermore, glassware, enamels, jewelry, and textiles at every turn demonstrate to the traveler in the East the capacity for imaginative forms. Oriental pictures are not infrequently executed on screens. Moreover, the decorative so-called Japanese prints, so very popular with European and American artists, are produced semi-mechanically, at little cost, because of the possibility of satisfying by this means the demands of great numbers of people. Oriental art, unfortunately, has never widely impressed the great masses of the western world. While its symbolism is naturally foreign to us, we have no excuse for failing to appreciate its beauty.

The student of art, while he may be convinced of the high achievements of his own civilization, should not be unmindful that the arts of the ancient civilizations of Europe and Asia, as well as those of Mexico and Honduras, offer constant surprises and unending pleasure.

III

THE UTILITARIAN BASIS—THE UNIVERSALITY
OF ART

If we are to lay a liberal foundation for an appreciation of
the æsthetic expressions of a people, we must recognize the
true function of art within a civilization and the relation between art and the life it reflects. The true greatness of any
civilization has always been measured in terms of art. In
fact, art furnishes us the visible symbols of the aspirations of
a race. All records that we possess today of ancient civilization, it may be affirmed once more, belong largely to the
realm of art.

Because of the preponderance and accessibility of historical
examples of art as we find them assembled in museums and
galleries, many people are devoted to the study of art only in
its historical sense, as giving us representations of a bygone
period; and if they attempt the practice of any of the arts,
they not infrequently turn to a copying of classical forms.
The æsthetic problems of present-day civilization should,
rather, be approached in the spirit of the Greeks, with due
regard for the laws which have transcended time, and should
not be reduced to a matter of slavish imitation.

The æsthetic problem—the creation of beauty—has remained the same throughout the ages; but the expression of
the problem in present-day civilization should not be limited
to an imitation of forms of the past. The creating of monumental architecture has stirred artists of all civilizations; but
an American bank need not necessarily be fashioned like the
Parthenon.

The study of the classic formulas is of incalculable disci-
plinary value in the student atelier; but when it is persisted in

and practiced merely as a lifeless rule, it becomes meaningless. Real art can arise only from a real, living problem, independent of historical prejudice; it cannot result from a repetition of a historical formula. In many respects the art of our country has only begun to assert its native force,—only just dared to throw off the restraint of historic influences under which it has labored, unable for a long time to realize its own impulses. The art of the Greek was based on a noble civilization, a young and vigorous state. When Greek art was bodily transplanted to Italy, however, it did not thrive and develop as at home, because it was borrowed, and grafted on an alien root. Moreover, the Roman did not exercise his creative instinct as did the Greek, to carry on to higher individual Roman expression what had come from a people only slightly related. It is true that the decorative element in architecture and sculpture was much accentuated during the Roman period; classic simplicity, however, was sacrificed for ornateness, not always to the advantage of the work of art.

Many claim that the art of the Renaissance in Europe, the greatest since that of the Greeks, developed upon a foundation of the classic tradition. While this contention is partly tenable, the art of the Renaissance is attributable largely to that same spirit of spontaneous creative desire which existed among the Greeks and which again caused our modern movement in art, having its beginning, in fact, in the useful and decorative arts. The spirit of independence, the desire to avoid the standard forms of the past, arose simultaneously in the so-called fine and applied arts; for, as the Egyptians and the Greeks clearly show, many art forms are the result of the study of natural phenomena.

In the Renaissance we find, again, proof of the necessity for individual creative genius in a people that is to produce true art. The artistic A B C, so to speak, in architecture and sculpture, after having once been laid down by the Greeks (possibly by the Egyptians), has remained very much the same during the ages. There is little difference in the artistic formula of the Greek, of the old Roman, and of the Renaissance artist; but the spirit, the enthusiasm, the temperament, of the great Greek masters are recognized again in the leaders of the Renaissance, while it was lacking in the borrowed art of the Romans. Renaissance art was not merely a physical, imitative revival of old forms, or a direct transplanting of their artistic products, such as took place in the second century B.C.

© Ewing Galloway

VENETIAN RENAISSANCE PALACES
The Ca' d'Oro in the center

in Rome, but something quite different. It was a desire to realize an æsthetic ideal evolving directly out of local conditions. The Venetian architect of the sixteenth century could not copy any palaces from Greek models to line his canals, for those models would not fit his needs; nor could he appropriately shape his sculpture after great patterns of the past. It was the creative spirit which had guided a Phidias that now guided a Michelangelo, a Leonardo, and a Raphael. In the work of Leonardo, indeed, we have a perfect example of the all-pervading spirit of art. In his letter to Ludovico Sforza, after dwelling on his capacity as military engineer and his ability to construct cannon and scaling-ladders and mortars and engines of beautiful and useful shape, he concludes: "In time of peace I believe I can equal anyone in architecture in constructing public and private buildings and in conducting water from one place to another. I can execute sculpture, whether in marble, bronze, or terra cotta, and in painting I can do as much as any other, be he who he may. Further, I could engage to execute the bronze horse in eternal memory of your father and the illustrious house of Sforza."

It is this ability to turn every humble object, as if by magic, from something without meaning, without form, into something beautiful that characterizes the true artist. It is the universality of application of art principles which alone can transform a country from a pseudo-artistic state into a civilization of true artistic significance. Isolated artistic expressions may exist by accident, but the feeling of artistic unity will never spring from too narrow a base.

The Renaissance shines in the brilliance of its many versatile artists who were never too proud to turn their hands to the beautification of things of common use. As with the Greeks, here too the beautiful and useful went hand in hand. The deplorable relegation of, shall we say, "unfine" artists to a lesser category is the failing of the present age. Many of the so-called artists of the Renaissance might with much justification be called artisans today, by reason of the practical uses to which their work might be put, although in quality it is superior to that of many modern so-called artists. Do not let us forget that Benvenuto Cellini made a masterpiece of a salt-cellar and that Niccolo dell' Arca modeled a candelabrum (see frontispiece).

Obviously, we are not as yet fully applying our inherent art instinct in the United States to the artistic treatment of utilitarian objects. At the St. Louis Exposition in 1904, the most fascinating art was not all found in the Fine-Arts Palace, but in another building devoted to the so-called minor arts, where certain complete units, from carpets to pictures, were exhibited in harmonious relationship. In San Francisco in 1915, the matter of grouping applied and fine arts together was officially under consideration, but at the last moment it was decided that such a logical arrangement was impossible. Still, as many remember, this was done in part; for several of the foreign nations, under no restrictions as to the management of their art exhibitions, and following a custom now well established abroad, did not confine their exhibits exclusively to pictures, and they thus saved the Palace of Fine Arts from what would have been monotony. Japan had wonderful screen pictures, bronzes, carvings, lacquer ware, and all the practical art of the Orient, upon which we ourselves are beginning to focus our attention. China exhibited similar things. Sweden provided decorative pictures made into wall hangings, and France, in a building all by herself, charmed thousands of people daily with a most ingenious combination of the fine and the applied arts. A people who can give such æsthetic pleasure by a neighborly display of Gobelins, perfumes, porcelains, and pictures justly deserves our unstinted praise.

In the American section the only worker in the useful arts was Mr. Louis Tiffany, who was represented by some excellent jewelry and decorative vases. As for the rest of the exhibition, it was a veritable ocean of paintings.

To correct this limited attitude is perhaps our most important problem in art education. Why do we not more generally recognize as real or potential expressions of art good architecture of every kind, fountains, mural decorations, furniture, ceramics, garden effects, and the thousand real things capable of artistic formulation and expression? The great artist of bygone periods, whether architect or sculptor, would sometimes smile at the topsy-turviness of our modern art, which indulges in distinctions not always based upon convincing reasoning. Not only is the layman guilty of misconception as to what constitutes art, but very frequently artists themselves show condescension rather than pride when they turn their talent toward basic utilitarian art. They are, in fact, likely to do this only after having made a failure of so-called higher creative aspirations. The artist who begins with purely creative aspiration, but who, failing in that lofty aim, then turns to a craft for a livelihood, is often a good illustration of inverted methods of modern art.

The only logical way to cope with the great desire of our people to limit their appreciation of art to one form—namely, painting—is, for example, to teach them first to appreciate the beauty of a well-designed spoon, proceeding then, in an evolutionary way, from practical things without an inner meaning to things of a more detached artistic expression, such as sculpture or easel painting. Artists themselves should be trained along this line, for the old-fashioned evolution from artisan to artist has not lost its logic today. In other words, to learn to appreciate in the right way the principles involved in painting or so-called higher forms of art, one may begin at the bottom of the ladder, and learn to see beauty and get æsthetic enjoyment out of ordinary useful things. A person who really understands art as a principle cannot fail to understand the artistic qualities of a well-designed spoon. However, those in a position to know are not convinced that this is true in the case of very many people who profess to derive pleasure from the study of pictures.

Among our professional artists there may be observed, however, a most hopeful symptom in the constantly increasing employment of our sculptors and painters in what they themselves, unfortunately, often term commercial work. Peculiarly enough, it is often their most significant work, because it is the kind which has a logical foundation. Fortunately, also, our easel painters are coming more and more into contact with practical necessities, particularly in the field of interior decoration and illustration. The protest that William Morris voiced for his time in England should be appreciated in our own country. His plea for an art that should concern itself with the fundamental necessities was well founded, and he

A CHRISTMAS FESTIVAL IN HEAVEN

Modern wood-carving by John Kirchmayer. (Detroit Museum, Detroit)

initiated a movement in that direction which seems likely to supersede the specialization which has prevailed since the decline of the Renaissance.

The temptation to go along the beaten path is too obvious not to lure a great many artists. It is much more convenient, less exacting in every sense, endlessly to repeat historic ornament. Yet to what disastrous consequences this never-ending repeating of old artistic forms may lead is well illustrated in the case of the acanthus. In an arid country like Greece it was one of the few indigenous forms presenting itself to the architect-designer for decorative purposes. The Greeks made use of it, as in the Corinthian order, understanding fully its wonderful constructive possibilities; and the Romans used it with even greater decorative force. On its reappearance in the Renaissance it is still recognizably appropriate, though often merely copied as an almost abstract ornament. From that period on, its use in northern Europe became more and more imitative, and eventually much of its real character was lost, until at present one has the feeling that, particularly during the end of the last century, many architects, sculptors, and decorative designers simply copied it in never-ending monotony, having no opportunities to observe its growth in nature, since it is not indigenous to northern Europe. And, like the acanthus, many other foreign motifs have become meaningless as treated in the work of artists.

Convincing artistic expression has always rooted in personal experience, derived from local problems and needs. No matter how clever the design may be, it must possess the spirit of the natural objects. Every imitation in architecture and furniture that is thoughtlessly copied from an earlier period suffers from the absence of real underlying experience; for no matter how well done, it is generally devoid of that conviction which is essential in good art.

The motives of the Renaissance artists who resented the introduction of Gothic art into Italy were simple enough. While they may have recognized its beauty, they must have felt that such architecture—such steep roofs, such fragile, lacy walls—was not well adapted to southern-European conditions. Again, the decorative forms of the Gothic were all foreign to Italian eyes. The oak and the maple were Northern, and the sympathies of the Italians were all with the palm and the laurel and the olive. Therefore classical architecture today largely prevails in the lands of its origin, while Gothic has gained its strongest foothold in France, Germany, and England.

RESIDENCE OF MR. TEMPLETON CROCKER, SAN MATEO, CALIFORNIA

A work of modern architecture of classic beauty, combining strength with elegance. The space relation of the three stories is most agreeable to the eye. The horizontal emphasis of the structure creates a marked sense of repose. (Willis Polk, architect)

In our country, architecture is almost entirely governed by classic precepts, although other historic styles are not without their followers. Who does not contemplate with some disappointment the innumerable replicas of the Pantheon or of the dome of St. Peter's, which since earliest days have been the architectural motifs of many state capitols and county seats from the Atlantic to the Pacific coast? Is such indulgence in mechanical repetition due to a lack of originality among our architects, or is it more an academic adherence to a universally admired standard form? Many of our American public buildings are very lofty and of noble proportions, their practical purpose being to serve as the physical emphasis of the center of the city's business. But as these Renaissance domes are largely ornamental, their architects need not have been hampered by any practical requirement in their construction. Hence some new form, sprung from a new opportunity, might have been substituted. Some domes, like that of the Capitol at Washington or of the new San Francisco City Hall, are very beautiful in their fine proportions, their well-ordered ornamentation, and their successful personal note,—the note which alone can save such buildings from being commonplace. In some cities, particularly abroad, this problem has, however, been solved with much greater originality. A recent evidence of independent thinking is the new design by Bertram Grosvenor Goodhue for the State House in Nebraska.

Architecture, as the mother or, perhaps, the foster mother of several arts, is the governing factor in a great variety of artistic activities; for the sculptor, the painter, the decorator, are constantly looking to her for new opportunities. It is true that we have the skyscraper as our original architectural contribution. The older type of skyscraper was not always beautiful in proportion, but some of the latter-day towers, particularly the Woolworth Building (conceived in the Gothic style), are exceedingly beautiful as masterpieces of rhythm. Collectively, however, to one standing among them in lower New York, although impressive in their mass effect, they are very ineffective decoratively.

Our engineers are solving many problems with some regard for artistic proportion; many modern engineering feats of this country are both original and artistic. The use of concrete and steel in dams, bridges, buildings, and power houses is judicious from the artistic point of view. A bridge like the Lindenthal span over the East River is a wonderful example of proportion of rhythmic space-and-line work, and it will bring us more praise from competent art critics in Europe than many of our more usual expressions of art. The American engineer

is on the right track in developing a profession which heretofore has never been even recognized as an art, and which has
existed only as a necessary adjunct to architecture, often losing
its identity under an architectural cover. However, even now,
engineering schools, while they are conscious of the importance of structural design involving æsthetic principles, leave
the cultivation of the æsthetic largely to personal intuition.

In our decorative arts we can hardly be expected to have
done better than the European artist whose revival began with
the *art nouveau*. Our jig-saw ornamented buildings of the
seventies are not more offensive than similar European buildings of the same time; but the planing-mill-machinery ornament has had its day. The healthy growth of the new
decorative-art movement abroad has already spread to and
taken root here in America. We are definitely beginning to
recognize art in all things. We are actually beginning to ad-
vertise exhibitions of the "useful arts," a term that is meant to
denote the work of the useful artists, in contradistinction to
that of the "useless arts" by the useless artists. We cannot
escape the logic of this curious classification of art.

By the end of the last century, art in Europe and America
had become so surfeited with thoughtless imitation of historic
styles that the only course that promised any relief appeared
to be a return to the artistic shaping of humbler things. Picture-
making had lost sight of its true aims of representation and
design. The Düsseldorf and Munich schools flourished in
anecdotal pictures which had no relation to the sister arts of
architecture and sculpture, having invaded instead, in their
treatment of subject, the realm of literature.

Originating in England under William Morris, the new impulse for the beautification of everyday things spread to the
Continent—first to Belgium, where it was cultivated by Van der
Velde, and then to Germany and Austria; and soon the modern
movement spread all over Europe. Its progress was most
rapid, and it caused many local artistic revolutions. The "new
art" aimed first of all to be original, independent of the forms

of the past. The older generation of artists insisted that this was not possible, pointing with pride to the example of the Renaissance and its apparent imitation of Greek and Roman motifs.

We must find ourselves. The problem of artistic self-realization is the same to a nation as to an individual, and can be achieved only through a response in this new world of ours

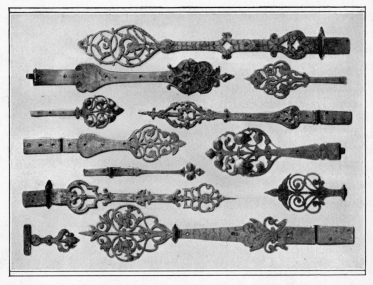

GERMAN-RENAISSANCE METAL HINGES
From the collection of the University of California

to the many new forms in nature available for ornamental purposes and also in the exploitation of the native raw materials of wood, stone, and marble. The possibilities in this direction in a new country like America are bewildering. There is the development of expression of constructive beauty; as, for instance, in the very modest "mission" furniture. It refrains from using any period forms of European origin. It is content to be devoid of any meaningless embellishments,—just plain American. It will always be in style, because it depends solely on good proportion and fitness. But one thing we can claim for it is that it did not result from any foreign motifs. It is a typical product of America, by reason of its sound construction, simplicity, and practical usefulness,—features that might have been brought out by an engineer. If it seems rigid, even crude, we must remember that its lack of sophistication is consistent with American civilization as a whole.

Art, then, expressed in formal perfection, must exist, must express itself, in every conceivable part of our physical surroundings. The fundamental requirement of an enormous amount of art is necessity. Art in its highest form—where it is concerned with the expression of emotion or passion—appeals to our æsthetic sense through purely formal qualities. One cannot emphasize this too much in the light of a common predilection for objects which are not expressive of an idea nor beautiful nor useful. The great art of any day must offer, as it does in many pictures, clear insight into the civilization upon which it is based. It must become the truthful record by which future generations may judge the humaneness of their forefathers. Therefore an art which shows merely skill in imitation can never be really alive; it will be impressive only as a feat.

Although the loftiest exemplification of art is, to the average person, the painting, it is to be hoped that all good citizens will, in time, extend their interest to other forms of artistic expression. This is our most urgent need. The art sections of our civic organizations and clubs, when they devote themselves to art, are no longer inclined to take up the study of painting—of Renaissance Madonnas. An art lecture at a club is now likely to mean a discussion of other art objects than pictures. Misgivings are no longer evident when it is suggested that the program be devoted to the subject of the beautification of the home garden, or to the problems of sculpture or even of mural decoration, to say nothing of architecture. While painting, poetry, and music are rightly regarded as the most exalted expressions of the noblest—spiritually, the most uplifting—elements in art, we must not forget that they are abstract art expressions, unrelated to anything we need and use in the practical affairs of life.

Pictures, then, either as the complete expression of the art of a people or as of fundamental educational value for the masses, are not the only evidences of the artistic standards of a nation. If we had consistently developed our art along the lines of our fundamental instincts, we should probably never have arrived at the making of transportable pictures, such as we now see by the thousands in art shops, exhibitions, and galleries generally, and for which we can never hope to stimulate any immediate use. One can only hope that the character of our art exhibitions will change radically so as to include all the manifestations of art which contribute to the beautification of even the humblest dwellings. In thus depriving art of its exclusive character as a luxury, we shall make it an alleviating factor in our life, free from the taint of decadence and arid privilege. The important problem before us is to spread the enjoyment of art broadly over our common world. Every material object in our country—even the walls and dwellings—will some day reflect, let us hope, the desire of men to make these objects alike beautiful and useful. We have in recent years made such prodigious beginnings in this country in developing the artistic significance of our dwellings that we have cause to think that we shall rank with the leaders in domestic architecture of the future. In fact, present-day American homes are on the whole more tastefully furnished than those of Europe. A sense of simplicity and fitness, and a demand for the practical, have saved America from some of the mistakes of the Old World, which has never been able to free itself completely from the meaningless imitation of historic styles.

That art as related to life does not always find its expression through the medium of the picture is shown abundantly by the great number of people of artistic instincts who seldom come in contact with paintings. Most of us have had the delightful

A MODERN WRITING DESK

The beauty of this desk lies in its happy proportions. Close examination will reveal a fine feeling for minor forms, particularly in the moldings and in the diminishing scale of the glass knobs

experience of meeting with all the qualities of an artistic atmosphere in the most unexpected and remote places, particularly those where there was no outward indication of that wealth which is usually at fault whenever people are tempted to acquire more than the necessary things. Good proportion, fine tonality, agreeable spacing and grouping of furniture, proper accentuation of color, often seem to work together, in

TAPROOM IN BUCKMAN TAVERN, LEXINGTON, MASSACHUSETTS

such instances, to produce a unity of artistic atmosphere, although the presence of paintings in such houses is not the rule but the exception.

Our national heritage of art, modest as it is in quantity, is of no mean quality artistically. In the very early days of American life we produced many things of practical use which never fail to charm the visitor to our modern museums in which the colonial room has been perpetuated. Colonial architecture was thoroughly congruous with our unsophisticated civilization, and its plain qualities are being revived today as typical of American ideals. Colonial furniture, textiles, pottery, and metal and glass utensils possess enjoyable qualities which were lost in the Victorian period. Modern perfection of machinery for the mass production of many articles was a severe blow to the arts, in that the hand-made article could not compete in price with the cheaper, machine-made substitute, for which extraordinary claims of perfection were readily made and accepted. As in the case of the boasts which were made for photography as offering a substitute for the graphic arts, the machine-made utilitarian object has not proved its claim to replace permanently the efforts of the craftsman.

IV

THE SCOPE AND CLASSIFICATION OF THE ARTS

While the term "art" was at one time applied only to the so-called fine arts, the scope of its use among enlightened people today has been so widened as to include all the activities which are productive of beauty in any form. The diversified manifestations of the arts in modern times have led to a paradoxical situation in the vocabulary of art. One hears of the fine arts, the æsthetic arts, the independent arts, the representative arts, the industrial arts, the minor arts, the lesser arts, the decorative arts, the applied arts, the useful arts. The nomenclature of art is thus elaborate and confusing. Let us inquire for a moment into the justification for these distinctions. As to the fine arts, there can be no doubt that all art is fine. If it is not fine,—that is, if it has not excellence, perfection, beauty,—it ceases to be art. The term "fine arts," though it rightly includes all the other classifications, is unfortunately limited, in the traditional sense, to reference to those arts independent of a utilitarian restriction. On the other hand, we carefully avoid the term "unfine arts," referring to the arts not included in the above list of the fine arts as the minor arts or the lesser arts, the applied arts or the industrial arts, the decorative arts or the useful arts. For all practical purposes the term "applied arts" covers all these other forms. One cannot escape, however, the conclusion that if the applied arts are the useful arts (which we cannot deny, certainly, as they do a practical work), the fine arts must be judged useless. In view of the disproportionate amount of energy and material used in the field of the so-called fine arts, their uselessness has become a serious problem in modern society. Because the applied arts are subservient to some practical use,—because of their being harnessed to the ordinary requirements of life,—they are sometimes excluded from the proud circle of the fine arts.

While one cannot deny the existence of this dividing line between freedom from practical requirements, on the one hand, and practical restrictions governed by utility, on the other, the rigid separation of the two groups of arts is, on the

ANCIENT GREEK VASES

These vases, of much variety of form, disclose the ingenuity of the Greek craftsman in creating beauty in utilitarian objects. Mythological and martial subjects, as well as subjects of everyday life, were used in the decoration with great
simplicity and effectiveness. (From the collection of the University of California)

whole, unfortunate and misleading. A perfect symbolic statue on a grave has no more æsthetic meaning than our modern American Lincoln penny. Greek vases made to carry water, wine, and oil have never been surpassed by the most beautiful work of modern ceramic workers. It is instructive to contemplate the many beautiful utilitarian objects which, having been rendered useless by injury, as in the case of a cracked vase, are admired when exhibited behind the plate glass of a museum display case. The distinction between "useful" and

"useless" art emphasizes the need for closer coöperation of all the arts. Many industrial arts or useful arts not only are undoubtedly dependable in giving a livelihood to those engaged in them, but also give abundant opportunity for æsthetic creative expression of a formal sort. Indeed, discrimination between the fine arts and the useful arts is not based on formal beauty, but rather on the additional power that the so-called fine arts possess because of their power of representing appearances.

In modern times, fortunately, we have again learned to recognize art in very many of the utilitarian objects through which human nature may gratify its sense of beauty; and although the arts, historically, are divided into the independent and the dependent arts, this classification should be no hindrance to the enjoyment of art in every form. The independent arts are the æsthetic, or fine, arts, particularly the representative arts (embracing architecture, sculpture, and painting), and also poetry, drama, music, and the dance. They exist largely for their own sake, for the sake of making an emotional appeal based upon their power of description. The dependent arts —landscape gardening, interior decoration, ceramics, goldsmithery, and others—minister primarily to some utilitarian purpose. It is undeniable that very many other activities are capable of the development of artistic qualities, and one hears in ordinary parlance of the acrobatic artist, the pyrotechnic artist, even the tonsorial artist; in fact, many a tailor craves to give himself an æsthetic halo. One cannot deny that etymologically the German word for "art," *Kunst*, is related to the verb *können*, "to be able," and that every activity which rises above the purely mechanical involves a certain amount of intelligence and instinctive talent. Wherever it is desirable to emphasize the difference between creative expression involving imaginative emotion and that governed by mere technical skill, we speak in the first instance of the creative artist and in the second of the artisan.

To most people the moving forces in their enjoyment of

poetry, painting, or sculpture are not the formal elements in the work or art, but rather the intellectual satisfaction which they derive from contemplating the subject matter. To the great majority of people the beauty of pure form, line, balance, symmetry, spacing, color, composition, is of little or no consequence, because they are often unable to appreciate these elements. Their approval of a picture or of a statue is based largely on the acceptability of the subject matter, which, if intelligible and, better yet, of a moralizing, didactic tone, is the decisive factor in causing them to pronounce favorably on it as a work of art. It is on account of its story-telling power that painting, the least abstract art in comparison with music and poetry, has come to transcend, in popular favor, all the other arts. On the other hand, the utilitarian object—an Oriental rug, for instance—does not necessarily possess the quality of moving our intellect by descriptive symbols; but it may bear infinitely more of real art meaning than many a poorly designed story-telling picture.

In the main we can recognize among the so-called independent, or fine, arts two definite groups: first, those arts which are expressed in space—architecture, plastic art, and painting; and, second, those which are expressed in time—music, drama, and literature, particularly poetry. In the former group the work of art is complete at once and forever. In the latter group the creation as it proceeds disappears, and a continued form of creation carries it on to completion.

Some of these arts may be enjoyed primarily through the visual and others through the auditory sense; although, in some, other senses help toward the enjoyment. The sense of touch, for instance, enters into the enjoyment of sculpture or textiles. Those arts which are comprehended by vision are architecture, sculpture, painting, and the dance, and also the decorative or applied arts. They represent by far the largest field for æsthetic enjoyment. Music and poetry appeal through the sense of hearing. The drama appeals to both vision and hearing. Ordinarily the visible, as compared with the audible,

A PERSIAN COURT CARPET OF THE SIXTEENTH CENTURY
From the collection of ex-Senator Clark, New York

arts are recognized as the most important,—the visible arts, as a general rule, seeming to lay people the more desirable ones. While all the arts aim at a very definite achievement, the promotion of æsthetic enjoyment, they are very different in

sidered desirable in painting; in fact, plasticity of expression we rightly expect of all the arts.

In painting, in marked contrast to both architecture and sculpture, the lines and forms are not tangible, but only visible. Although practiced as decoration from the dawn of history, painting developed as an independent representative art only

THE GLEANERS
By Jean François Millet. (The Louvre, Paris)

centuries after the finest flower of architecture and sculpture had wilted. Now, however, the great flexibility of technical expression in painting, and its power to give pleasure through the highly sensuous appeal of color, have given it first place in popular favor. The subjects capable of representation in painting are so numerous that its content appeal to the layman is its most potent force. Among the other important factors of enjoyment in painting are color and form, considered by some moderns as even more important than content.

Among the collected definitions of the art of literature contained in Gayley and Scott's well-known "Literary Criticism" we find, first, the following: "All knowledge that reaches us through books is literature." This indicates the wide scope of literary art, while the quality of this art is indicated in a second quotation: "The written thoughts and feelings of intelligent men and women arranged in a way that shall give pleasure to the reader is literature." We recognize from these definitions that the formal aim in literature is precisely the aim of painting and sculpture and music. Painting and sculpture are able only to present a single instant of an action at one time, while literature and music are able to carry on through an extended period the most elaborate set of actions.

It will be seen from these sketched outlines of the character of several different arts that the aim in every one is the achievement of formal beauty. Of this every art student must eventually be convinced.

V

NATURE AND ART—IMITATION OR INTERPRETATION

In all the arts, we may readily observe that artistic creation is dependent upon the material furnished by the external world; even the fantastic, the imaginary, as we shall see, is in its boldest flights directed by the guideposts of nature. The original stimulus for every work of art may be invariably traced to natural facts and phenomena.

Everywhere in art do we observe at least some elements provided by nature. This obvious truth has caused many to believe that the function of art is to be found in the imitation of nature. The idea has persisted since Aristotle, one of the very first to express ideas about art; and since he himself conceived the aim of art to be imitation of nature, one must not be surprised to find the idea in the minds of many less profound persons today. However, if we are to understand Aristotle correctly, we shall have to bear in mind that *imitation* to him meant *representation* in an interpretative sense. Who has not heard the myth about Zeuxis and Parrhasius, and their imitative rivalry—how the former so realistically painted a still-life that birds were tempted to peck; and how the latter, to go his colleague one better, painted a curtain which deceived the other into attempting to move it back to discover what was behind! It is a most interesting fact that this charming ancient myth has been one of the causes of the difficulties of the layman in his relation to art. Aside from this historical bias, we must recognize the reluctance of the average person to question the absolute authority of nature,—a reluctance due perhaps to the fact that nature has been a potent force in religion ever since man first tried to explain her perplexing mysteries. The artist, above all, surely would not be guilty

45

of a lack of respect for nature; for is it not he who recognizes nature as defying the gifts of man? The true artist humbly admits that nature may indeed create effects to which he is utterly incapable of doing justice. The glory of the heavens has been equaled only at times, in the works of Turner and Inness; while such gigantic spectacles as the Yosemite Valley and the Grand Cañon are artistically as yet unsolved. Artists themselves, unintentionally perhaps, have added to the common misunderstanding of the relation of art to nature, particularly when the meaning of their words has been taken too literally or too superficially. Every true artist constantly urges upon his students the need for the closest communion with nature.

Schiller as a poet has given us a suggestive concept of the relation of art to nature by saying that the poets are the guardians of nature. Nature, he says, is the flame which fires the soul of the poet; out of nature alone does he derive his whole power. All other artists will readily confess the same debt to nature. But from the time of Aristotle on, there has been no unanimity of opinion with respect to this relation; for, while in later times (particularly in Baumgarten, the originator of the term "æsthetics") Aristotle has found adherents to his often misinterpreted ideal of imitation, on the whole, however, the greater number of artists and critics find their attitude expressed in that of Hippolyte Taine, who prefers to think that art is imitative indeed, but that it must under no circumstance copy nature literally. "We expect rightly," he says, "that a statue should have correct proportions, executed with anatomical knowledge; in short, that it must resemble a human being. But that is not all. Otherwise the plaster cast made directly from nature would be the most artistic sculpture, a colored photograph would be the finest painting, and the stenographic report of a court proceeding would be the best literary creation." What artist,—he properly asks,—no matter how gifted, could compete for accurate detail with a sensitive photographic plate?

THE WHISTLING BOY

A splendid example of characterization achieved by concentration upon essentials. Painted by Frank Duveneck. (Cincinnati Museum)

Undoubtedly imitation has its place in art, however low a place it may be; this is obviously true, particularly if one considers that the apprentice invariably begins with imitation as his aim. He is at first engrossed with the problem of committing facts to memory by the process of copying them assiduously; but only when these facts, as he copies them, become endowed with superior qualities may he claim to be a true artist. While the copying of nature may contribute to the development of skill, it is hardly art in the highest sense.

What is, then, in practice, the process followed by the artist in his contact with nature when he endeavors to express himself in his particular medium? Looking at large numbers of paintings or works of sculpture in any exhibition, many people seem to feel that painters themselves differ very widely in that respect, as indeed they do. Curiously enough, however, the painters who, according to the profession, are lacking in artistic merit are frequently the choice of the public. The innovators in the artistic profession are not always recognized as true artists by the public until after the trusted connoisseur has spoken; and even then many naturally persist in their own preference. What the great mass of people think about an unexplained collection of works of art we very well know; indeed, we have some positive evidences in the results of the popular voting contests frequently held throughout the country in art galleries offering exhibits of recent works of art. The greatest number of votes not uncommonly goes to some imitative, photographic picture, while the real work of art—the one with a lasting quality of universal appeal—is often overlooked.

Very many paintings, then, are not art in the highest sense, but merely clever technical imitations of a fact, rendered correctly, perhaps, but without a fragment of suggestive power or of those finer elements that open avenues of beauty and give the thrills of æsthetic enjoyment which can be stimulated only by an imaginative and creative artist. Unfortunately, very many so-called artists, by reason of temperamental shortcomings, see the world just as the multitude see it,—a fact which often accounts for their popularity; the susceptible, imaginative artist, on the other hand, leaves the mere physical fact far behind him and soars above the heads of the crowd in the expressions of his imaginative fancy. To keep up with the former is obviously not a hard task, but the number of those privileged to accompany the latter is dependent upon an understanding of the higher ideals in art. The popular artist, then, is not invariably the good artist, nor is the unsuccessful artist necessarily devoid of good qualities in his work. The final verdict will always be passed by time.

Art deals, in its most interesting expressions, let us say again, with fancies, not facts. The real artist endeavors to lead us into an atmosphere which is distinctively of his own creation and which differs with every creative individuality. Only the creative artist who can bring to us things which are not an everyday feature of the world at large is capable of sustaining a permanent interest. All too frequent is the experience of the student who, after much painstaking toil over methods largely technical, thinks that all difficulties have now been conquered, and then finds himself face to face with the necessity of saying something in his acquired language. The number of those who paint well in a technical sense, who can reproduce a fact clearly, in paint dexterously employed, has always been large. But the company of the really creative painters, those of ideas, will always be limited. This earth, with all its many-sided aspects, its multicolored peoples, its illimitable fauna and flora, is open to all artists on the same basis. Only the gifted, however, will tell what they have seen and felt in such a way as to make their work vital, interesting, original, significant, and at the same time intelligible.

It is therefore important to learn that what we enjoy in nature as the picturesque and what the artist, on the other hand, considers paintable, must be recognized as two very different things. This fundamental fact is known to all artists: that there are phases of nature which are beyond the possibility of artistic expression. Because there are qualities, effects, and phenomena in nature which absolutely defy any known technical means at the command of the artist, they cannot be made available to others. The beginner, in his enthusiasm, is not always conscious of these limitations, and often, with great courage and devotion, he will attack a problem which experience has taught the master is not within his power to solve. After all, the sculptor uses only earth and stone and metal, and the painter employs colored pigments; these are the only materials at their command, to express the phenomena of nature. The musician cannot hope to rival thunder and lightning by any technical means at his disposal, and he has to be satisfied with a reduced scale to suggest these phenomena.

It is, then, the power of suggestion which makes a work of art convincing; but the physical imitation of realities is never conducive to this. One of the most grotesque examples of mistaken judgment regarding the limitations of art was afforded by a picture exhibited in Europe some years ago. This picture dealt with a Biblical motive, "The Jews worshiping the Golden Calf." It was an oil painting, true to its medium except for the golden calf, ensconced above the multitude. Instead of being painted, the calf was modeled in plastic relief and covered with gold leaf. But the result was not convincing in the least. Making golden sunsets more golden by using real gold on canvas, making beaches more sandy by putting sand on canvas, making fowl more feathery by attaching real feathers to the painted canvas, does not strengthen the illusion, but simply destroys it.

People in contact with the world of nature are at all times discovering enchanting vistas which, to their disappointment, do not stir the artist, and very often artists are puzzled over the jubilant descriptions of scenery which the art-loving layman advises them to paint. The true artist knows the limitations of his means, and he respects these limitations as an inevitable fact. The discerning artist turns to simple things. Waterfalls which thunder into his field of vision at one corner and impetuously rush out at another appeal to few artists as potential motifs for paintings. The sketching grounds for the landscape painter, here and elsewhere, have seldom been brought to his attention by the traveling public, but rather by his own instinct for nature suitably presented for his need in

THE WINDY DOORSTEP

Note the combination of movement and stability in the figure. Its realistic effect has been achieved with extraordinarily simple means. Sculptured by Abastenia St. Leger Eberle, New York

terms of character, simplicity, and true picturesqueness. St. Ives, Concarneau, Étaples, Laren, Volendam, Worpswede, Dachau,—to name a few such localities abroad,—would hardly be known if it were not for the artist. They become known in spite of the lack of public patronage. Here in America it has been the same. The virile character of the Maine coast, first expressed in such monumental simplicity by Winslow Homer; the tranquil charms of Woodstock, New York, now recognized in the work of so many of our successful pastoral landscape painters, are not discovered by those who travel the automobile highways. In the West artists turn rarely to the Canadian Rockies, the great mountains of the Northwest, the Yosemite, Lake Tahoe, or other popular beauty spots. They feel that the natural phenomena presented at such localities are not, ordinarily, within the means of expression of their art. They often retire to the placid beauty of Monterey Bay, Laguna Beach, the shores of Marin County, or the marshes of the great valleys. The desert, unpopular with the tourist, appeals to many artists strongly, no matter how disagreeable may be the associations connected with it. How many really lasting works of art can we point to which are based on subjects commonly spoken of as magnificent scenery? On the other hand, some of the most captivating and enduring of canvases are based on subjects which no layman would stop to look at if he saw them in reality.

In all fields of painting it is much the same. In figure painting, fashionable and expensively gowned women often appear trivial and uninteresting as compared with such paintings as Duveneck's ragged "Whistling Boy," in the Cincinnati Museum: he looks much more picturesque than a polished, characterless, stereotyped subject. It cannot be denied that artists have a way of turning toward the dilapidated, the ruined, the decayed, and it is no morbidness, either, which deflects their attention to these things. There is variety of form, of surface, of color, in an old weathered cottage, covered with moss and stains, which is lacking in a new building.

An example of the merely imitative type of painting is Church's well-known "Niagara," in the Corcoran Gallery at Washington. This picture aims at absolute fidelity to nature through accurate registration of facts. It is very doubtful, however, whether it achieves its aim of conveying the essential features of Niagara. The successful painters of all times have always recognized the necessity for dealing arbitrarily with

NIAGARA FALLS

From the painting by Frederick Edwin Church. (Corcoran Gallery of Art, Washington, D.C.)

facts and still preserving their telling points. Only the novice, the person of no insight, will attempt to transcribe any subject just as it presents itself. The landscapes which are attempted copies of nature are not satisfactory as works of art; they are devoid of everything that makes a work of art interesting. It is the power of selection, emphasis, subordination, and interpretation that has gone into a painting which determines its success or failure. Our great figure-painters also,—Whistler, Sargent, Chase, Tarbell, or any of those whose work seems so obviously correct and complete,—show obedience to these laws without any evident effort. In regard to portraiture the question is often asked, Is not photographic likeness the most essential requirement in a good portrait? It is; but what should we perceive likeness to be? The mechanical likeness produced by the lens is not satisfactory even to the commercial photographer. By means of a small retouching brush he makes his picture into something which pretends to be an improvement on nature; he idealizes it. (For the present we must be satisfied with this statement, postponing consideration of the problem of idealization until the next chapter. However, the subject of this chapter is inextricably bound up with that of the next.) The portrait is usually not a success if merely imitation in the literal sense. All great portraits are the result of a selective process; this is clearly demonstrated in any two portraits made of the same sitter by two different artists. It has been demonstrated in the history of art several times and may be observed not infrequently today in contemporary exhibitions. If both portraits are the work of two really gifted artists, the results may vary greatly without the sacrifice of what is called likeness. In painting or sculpture, then, likeness is some one outstanding, characteristic phase in personality as indicated in spiritual and formal values not realizable through mere imitations. In literature or the drama the varying expression of a personality may be portrayed in endless change. This, it should be remembered, is not possible in a painting or in sculpture.

Where is the landscape painter who has not been confronted with the well-meant question of the interested layman, "Where did you take this picture?" It was probably, if at all a good picture, not "taken" anywhere; perhaps it was not even painted outdoors but was largely the accumulated result of the artist's outdoor studies. These studies may consist of visual observation alone or of sketches,—the committing of these observations to paper or canvas by means of pencil or brush. Hardly any convincing painting, no matter what its

TANIS

This picture, by Daniel Garber, is conspicuous for its careful selection of detail
reduced to simple terms. It derives much charm from the management of the
light problem involved

subject may be, is true to nature in the imitative, photographic
sense. The very best we should expect of it is an external
approximation, æsthetically agreeable. It should, however, be
true to nature in spirit. It is, indeed, a significant day for

any enthusiast when he discovers that there is no foundation for his belief in literal imitation of nature in art. As early as the eighteenth century Reynolds, in his interesting discourses on art, pointed out to his students that general copying is a delusive kind of industry. "The student satisfies himself with the appearance of doing something; he falls into the dangerous habit of imitating without selecting, and of laboring without any determinate object. As it requires no effort of the mind, he sleeps over his work; and those powers of invention and disposition which ought particularly to be called out and put into action lie torpid and lose their energy for want of exercise. How incapable of producing anything of their own are those who have spent their time in making finished copies is well known to all who are conversant with art."

The intention to copy nature undoubtedly shows a laudable respect for the "mother of all the arts." The many attempts we may have seen here and there are of the most unsatisfactory kind. Nature, let us remember, is not always within the reach of artistic expression; and when she is, it should be the artist's aim to give her in his work that fullness of beauty which exists only in ideal form, in his own mind. Why duplicate something that already exists unless you can glorify it, visioning its most exalted possibilities?

It is the arbitrary selection and arrangement of the component parts of any picture upon the canvas which, while undoubtedly puzzling to the layman, is recognized by the artist as the first important evidence of his fellow artist's ability. Munkácsy, the Hungarian painter, who successfully covered large surfaces, painted even his very largest compositions, like "Golgotha," from memory. His numerous preliminary studies, his sketches, were not within his sight during his final work,—a fact that disproves the popular fallacy that a large picture is merely an enlargement of a small sketch. Our own painters, like George Inness and Francis Murphy, were most interesting examples of the ability to work independently and creatively in the absence of sketches or studies.

It is not so well-known a fact that the student in Chinese art schools is encouraged to look at his model, to study it intently, as long as he will. When he begins to paint, however, the model no longer is before him. In that way he remembers what is characteristic and forgets the unessential.

Many an artist has felt the difficulties of this problem in his contact with the public when sketching outdoors, particularly when his finished study, into which everything has been carried that is essential, elicits the unsophisticated question, "Of course, when you get home you will finish this?" Generally the tormented painter assents good-naturedly, since he is ready to grant any concession under these exasperating conditions. As a matter of fact, what the artist takes out of nature is only a limited number of elements, and these are the essential, the telling features which carry the point. He knows that if he should take everything there is before him, his picture would be nothing but nature crowded into a small canvas, while the effect he is really after is to maintain that feeling of harmony that is so uplifting in nature. Any layman who has ever watched a painter work, either indoors or out, is astonished to see how many things he omits and how many he apparently adds. Therefore the first thing the student should understand is the necessity on the part of the artist to make whatever arbitrary changes he sees fit, in order to attain balance, symmetry, harmony, and rhythm, and, in the end, that feeling of unity, of oneness, which is so essential in any great work of art, and which is not always present in nature.

What charms us in a picture is the artist's ability to seize upon the determining element of something he has observed and to present it to us in its simplest, most convincing, most characteristic, and most beautiful aspect. The entire range of human spiritual qualities may be reflected in figural and portrait work, while all the subtler shades of outdoor moods may enter into the appeal of a landscape. It must become clear, then, that the obviousness of a picture as an accurate representation of a fact is not an adequate test of its artistic worth.

HENRY G. MARQUAND

By John Singer Sargent. (Courtesy of the Metropolitan Museum of Art)

The qualities which the artist recognizes and which are the cause of æsthetic pleasure are demonstrable, and we shall deal with them more specifically in the following chapters.

A picture, to whatever type it belongs—portrait, figure, landscape, or genre—is a complete unit in itself. Its relation to the wall upon which it hangs forces restrictions upon it of which we are not conscious in nature. Every work of art is an arbitrary *arrangement*, and this fact at once gives it freedom of expression. If it were merely a slavish imitation, it would be lacking in all the vital appeal which comes with the intelligent application of rules.

A work of art, then, is essentially the result of selection, and this process naturally involves the acceptance of some elements and the rejection of others. This statement alone should convince the student of the fallaciousness of the idea that art is a process of imitation. Sculpture and painting have for many a delusive fascination which arises out of their imitative element, and the public has sometimes insisted upon this element to such an extent that it has nearly spelled ruin to many an artist.

Often, it is true, the artist falls below the qualities of nature in his work; on the other hand, he may well equal nature, or, if he is an artist of real ability, he may glorify it. All great works of art surpass nature in the heightened expression of artistic quality. Art is the realization of the spirit of nature, —not merely a literal imitation of form,—and no work of art that has spiritual quality can be realized by mechanical copying: it must be the result of thoughtful selection and arrangement of the telling elements.

VI

IDEALISM VERSUS REALISM

That art to many people is so bewildering is due not only to the boundless variety of its manifestations but also to a prevailing ambiguity in the use of the term "beauty," commonly believed to represent the aim of art. To furnish a concise explanation of the word "art," even in a dictionary definition, the beginner usually finds very difficult; and one is reminded in this of the common predicament which follows the well-known query What is a spiral?—the movement of the hand being commonly the only answer. That is to say, many people know what is meant by "art" and can give examples to illustrate what they mean, but they falter in attempting any direct statement of the meaning of the term "beauty." To the artist himself the problem is much less embarrassing than to the layman, because he feels that what he creates is *ipso facto* art, by reason of his possession of a God-given talent for producing the thing we call art; and he is therefore ordinarily not concerned with terms and definitions. For the convenience of the public, and for philosophic purposes, "art" has been defined in many ways, all in the last analysis expressing the same idea. Art is essentially a means of "expression" designed to give æsthetic pleasure.

Beginning with the Greeks we can point to a long list of writers who have speculated upon the meaning of art; and the efforts toward a categorical statement of the meaning of beauty are the cause of a constantly increasing literature in the field of æsthetics. Aside from the question whether beauty may be created by the imitation of nature (a question taken up in the preceding chapter), the recognition of beauty in certain things, to the exclusion of others, as well as beauty as a prerequisite to art, are the cause of æsthetic discussions and dissensions.[1]

Among many definitions popular in the history of art, we find that "art is nature seen through the eyes of an artist"; and that Ruskin proclaimed that "art is the whole spirit of man." Van Dyke, a contemporary, says that "art is the mingling of nature and human nature." Another present-day writer claims that it is the concrete embodiment of an ideal, and Carleton Noyes interprets art as "the medium by which the artist communicates himself to his fellows." Ralph Adams Cram is pleased to call art "the symbolical expression of otherwise inexpressible ideas." To Santayana "art is a rehearsal of rational living, and recasts in idea a world which we have no present means of recasting in reality."

Like categorical statements in the case of all great truths of man, all these statements are partial and incomplete, although in their total meaning they undoubtedly cover many essentials of the subject. After all, we must not forget that, whether in book, picture, or statue, art is not only the thing expressed but also the manner of its expression. It is both in its ideas and in the language in which they are presented that we recognize art.

Granted that in the academic, traditional sense the aim of art is beauty, it becomes necessary to define this term as applied both to content and to the external form of a work of art.

In the academic sense the beautiful is a divine revelation, something which rises above the real nature of things as a superior truth. To the Greeks everything good is also beautiful and everything beautiful is also essentially good. Among them the beautiful and the useful also were identified in the popular mind. In the light of certain modern art developments we shall pay attention to a little later, this old standard has

[1] A most illuminating historical treatise on the theory of beauty is the "Philosophy of the Beautiful," by William Knight, in which an analysis of the chief theories of æsthetics may be found.

ceased to function among many artists. For the present we shall concern ourselves with the traditional, classic, or better, perhaps, academic concept of spiritual art values and reserve the more recent concepts of art to be discussed later.

According to those thinkers governed by classic precepts, the absolutely beautiful does not exist either in a work of art or in nature, because the absolutely beautiful is absolute æsthetic and moral perfection, which, according to religious theories, can be found only in the Creator. Every artist knows only too well how difficult it is to realize absolute perfection. Even where others praise his creation, he sighs before his work, realizing its imperfections. The true artist knows how far away even his most successful efforts are from the absolute ideal, the absolutely perfect.

From the following outlined scale of values, based upon academic concepts, it will be seen that the old idea of beauty has its basis upon *moral and physical perfection*. All feelings which rest in the violent passions are therefore unæsthetic,— in fact, are ugly,—because the ideally beautiful must have repose, depth, and an inner harmony,—qualities all foreign to passionate excitement. Physical imperfections, socially and ethically unacceptable ideas, were rejected as unfit for the highest expressions of art. In pursuing beauty it becomes, therefore, the problem of art to realize these highest æsthetic and ethical qualities.

The nearest to the divinely perfect in the academic sense we may recognize in the lofty, the great, the majestic,—in an expression of art which makes us stand in awe, in astonishment, as before a magnificent Gothic cathedral. The placid expanse of the ocean, the starry sky, gigantic mountains covered with snow, or the aspiring columns of a sequoia forest,—all these are things which stimulate this feeling of majestic grandeur in its highest expression.

On the other hand, storm and thunder, tremendous waterfalls, have the same majestic quality, combined, however, with motion. An earthquake which causes destruction of beauti-

ful realities, of sweet aspirations, has nothing of the lofty and
elevated in it, and therefore assumes the character of the

LA PIETÀ
By Michelangelo. (St. Peter's, Rome)

terrible. It lends itself to artistic presentation when tragedy, as
an art expression, is the aim. Such expressions as "magnificent
desolation" were frequently used in describing San Francisco

reduced to ashes in 1906. Greatness and loftiness are often the underlying motive for much that is admired in art. A truly great work of art, in the sense of the term indicated here, many artists aspire to produce; many of the greatest achievements in classic art approached the great, the magnificent, the lofty.

Lower in the academic scale of qualities in art we meet with the rich, the luxuriant, either in form or ideas. Other, minor qualities, however, are loveliness, charm, niceness, interest, pleasantness, gracefulness, tenderness—these are all qualities which agreeably affect us in art or in nature.

Any quality of body or mind suggesting physical defects or ethically objectionable is proportionately lower in the academic scale of importance as a subject of art. The graceful, the dainty, the tender, the charming, are not rated on a par with the splendid, the pompous, the impressive, the majestic, or the imposing, identified with whatever it may be, either in nature or in human affairs. At the bottom of the academic subject evaluation in art we find the comic, and inferior to it, even, the laughable, the contemptible. As an expression of human intelligence the comic is assigned a place near the bottom of the ladder.

Many artists of the present day, however, have rejected the academic requisite of moral and physical perfection. Kenyon Cox, who was thoroughly infused with classic ideals, felt that "the art of the past was produced for a public that wanted it and understood it, by artists who understood and sympathized with their public; the art of our time has been for the most part produced for a public that did not want it and misunderstood it, by artists who despised the public for which they worked."

There can be no doubt, if we are to judge art from the attitude of the average man, that he expects of art a glorified statement of his aspirations. Has not Ruskin himself stated his belief that all art is praise? The attainment of wealth, power, physical perfection, moral ideals of every kind, as expressed by all visible symbols intelligible to mankind, is still the ideal of the average person. Everything contributing or suggesting or representing comfort or happiness is the aim of the man in the street, and he clings tenaciously to the hope of the realization of this ideal; and if denied it in reality, he at least hopes to enjoy it in the abstract, through the medium of

DANCE OF THE NYMPHS
By Jean Baptiste Camille Corot. (The Louvre, Paris)

art. This ideal view, we shall learn, is objected to by those moderns who profess to see in life not a state of happiness and contentment but an existence made up of conflicts, disappointments, failures, and struggles. To them, accordingly, art should deal with the realities of life.

No art epoch, therefore,—so at any rate it appears to many, —has been so full of contradiction as that of our own time. If art truly reflects the main currents of life, this conflict of opinions of art at present will seem more understandable if we regard the World War as expressing the trend of modern society and its unfortunate complexities and mistakes. Art, in some respects no less than society, seems to many pessimists to have drifted toward an abyss from which many believe no escape is possible. The trend of modern art in its several

PORTRAIT OF MY MOTHER

By James McNeill Whistler. (Musée de Luxembourg)

aspects suggests that in many ways we of today have outgrown the academic ideals which guided the majority of artists through centuries.

It is clear that the attitude of many modern artists is assuredly not compatible with the academic ideals in art; and if we accept the theories of the idealist, who professes to recognize beauty only in morally acceptable ideas, it is a vain task to try to arrive at any satisfactory explanation as to the meaning and aims of expressions of art which differ in concept from the ideal. The futurist, whom we shall meet again in another chapter, openly asserted his radical disregard of all the theories and many of the practices of the academic schools, largely, by his own admission, out of despair over the futility of hoping to equal, much less surpass, the excellence of the older masters. The futurist, whatever we may think about his efforts, is therefore not to be judged in the light of any academic concepts. We cannot in all fairness object to his philosophy: man, with commendable ambition, wants to create new ideas and express them in new ways.

The exponents of "radical modernism" in all fields of art usually make the same claims: while they frankly admit that the subject matter in their work is unacademic, they insist that the form in which it is expressed is æsthetically significant. Here again, the question forces itself to the foreground, Can art have a one-sided perfection or must it present a unity of perfection of both content and form?

However, many moderns have only discarded the old-fashioned idealism, as expressed in subjects, in the hope of finding new vigor, and significant expression of the time in which they live. Being often acutely alive and ambitious, modern artists feel that there is nothing more interesting than the activities of their own society and its background. In order to achieve their aspirations, they have turned to the worship of realism and even naturalism. The realist and naturalist in art, we should explain here, are firm believers in the adequate value of all subjects as furnished by the life about them; they differ in the manner in which they formally treat their subjects. That is, the realist artistically alters the form, with the view of emphasizing the significance of the idea he seeks to present; the naturalist, on the contrary, is photographic,—he is content to give us the scene or the character in all its infinite unselected detail, and lets us make of it what we will.

The preoccupation with so-called undesirable subjects is not of recent date: it has been known since the beginning of art.

The modern realist has his classic prototype. Among the ancient Greeks we find Pauson and Pyreicus, two "naturalists." Even the Greeks, then, had such artists. It is true that they meted out to them strict justice. Pauson, who is said to have confined himself to the ordinary in nature and whose depraved tastes liked best to represent the imperfections and deformities of humanity, lived in the most abandoned poverty; and Pyreicus, "who painted barbers' rooms, dirty workshops, donkeys, and kitchen herbs as if such things were rare or attractive in nature, acquired the surname of 'Rhyparographer,' the dirt-painter."

Muther, a leading modern art historian, in discussing the subject matter of the modern French painters of realistic and naturalistic tendencies, presents the following inventory of subjects taken from Zola, which may well be considered appropriate to literature, as well as to painting. He says: "Everything is being painted: the machine shops, the depots, machinery halls, workshops, the glowing ovens of the smelting-works, official gala performances, salons, scenes of dramatic life, cafés, shops and masked balls, races and the stock exchange, clubs, baths, high-priced restaurants and eating-houses as well, banks, gaming-casinos, boudoirs, ateliers and sleeping-cars, lecture rooms in universities,—the whole of humanity, wherever it may be found and to whatever class it may belong, —at home, in the hospitals, at the cafés, in the theaters, and on the boulevards." One could extend this picture ad infinitum, but it will suffice to give an idea of the many-sidedness of the subject in realism.

In our day the advocates of absolute realism, devoid of any academic precepts, have cast all restraint to the winds. In painting, sculpture, literature, they parade their slogan "Whatever is, is; Life is Truth and Truth is Art." It is undeniable that a great portion of the public has become increasingly bewildered, even dismayed, and declines to enter into the controversy as to the relative merits of academic idealism and modernism. Many of those who do take sides, however, are

THE DRINKER

A realistic subject expressed in forceful technique, by Randall Davey. Whether
one approves of the subject or not, one must admit that the characterization
is excellent

still firmly convinced that the idealistic principle of art will
eventually win out. Is art at present a truthful mirror of the
best in life and does it give the average man what he calls
worth while? That is a question now asked by many. Be-

lievers in academic criteria, they profess to look in vain for noble or fine characters in many present-day realistic expressions of art; they fail to discover any sentiment reflecting the higher and better emotions of the human breast. The women, to them, in many modern literary works, appear to be pleasure-loving dolls without moral stamina. The men seem to them to

THE HIPPODROME

A realistic subject expressed in a very spontaneous manner, by Gifford Beal.
A marked feeling of the simultaneous activities of circus performances has been achieved without the suggestion of confusion

believe in nothing: they appear to be super-egoists devoid of ideals and aspirations,—hard, arrogant, and vicious. Particularly relative to certain modern works of literature, academic critics feel a very keen dissatisfaction with the modern realistic tendency in art. The revival of realism, doubtless, is an expression of modern times,—not of any individual. Realism began as a *fin de siècle* manifestation, which penetrated into society, science, literature and other arts, even into politics.

If we are to understand it, we must cast a glance at the situation which was caused in the seventies and eighties by the development of the natural sciences and the enormous emphasis put upon "facts." Furthermore, the social problem, the fight for existence, brought the working class into the limelight,

LOWER MANHATTAN
By Leon Kroll

and there followed emphasis on the proletarian subject in art. While the classic idea in art may be described as an aim at the godlike, the modern idea in certain instances may be described as aiming at the manlike.

Art, undoubtedly, with many moderns, ceases to be an object in itself. It has become revolutionary against academic traditions. A modern author, Sudermann, insists that *Poesie*, for instance, "is no longer a light, elegant tripping among beds of roses, not a cowardly play with agreeable sensations, not a stupid affection of dead symbols, but a serious coöperative power in the ideals of a new and growing art."

As in the case of the public, by no means all the artists of our time are in sympathy with the prevailing realistic tendencies. We may find many of them upholding the ideals of other days. For a very extreme view of modern tendencies, as seen through the dark glasses of a well-known reactionary, we must turn to Max Nordau, who, in a much-discussed volume, "Degeneration," presents a most alarming theory of the nature of realism, inspired by the now largely discredited ideas of Lombroso that degeneration among criminals is the result of inheritance. Nordau presents a voluminous dissertation in which he states that "degenerates are not always criminals, anarchists, and lunatics: they are often authors and artists. Some among these degenerates in literature, music, and painting have in recent years come into extraordinary prominence, and are revered by numerous admirers as creators of new art and heralds of coming centuries. This phenomenon is not to be disregarded. Books and works of art exercise a powerful suggestion on the masses. It is from these productions that an age derives its ideals of morality and beauty. If they are absurd and antisocial, they exert a disturbing and corrupting influence on the views of a whole generation. Hence the latter, especially irresponsible youth easily excited to enthusiasm, now must be warned and enlightened as to the real nature of the creations so blindly admired."

Nordau, then, fears that degeneration is the disease of the age, and he shows no hesitation whatever in classifying as degenerates such artists as Zola, Monet, Wagner, Tolstoy, Ibsen, Hauptmann, Walt Whitman. The slogans "Freedom," "Modernity," "Progress," "Truth," do not deceive him as to their ego worship and lack of discipline. He makes alarming statements which unfortunately furnish food for those who see in art only an agency for the bad.

Although the views of Nordau, expressed in the year 1893, seem extreme, the outcry against modern tendencies is sustained by similar protests expressed by some physicians and others against an exhibition, in 1921, of modernists' art at the Metropolitan Museum at New York.

Political and social reactionaries are likely to ascribe this expression of strident realism to the breakdown of the old social order, and they are tempted to put the blame at the feet of the "rising goddess Democracy." They maintain that under the aristocratic rule of the Old World the appreciation of art offered no such difficulties as today, since there was only one type of art, the prescribed idealistic form. It is self-evident that art never stands still; neither is it mastered by the limited experience of one generation—it transcends time.

The conflict between the academic idealist and the modern realist obviously is due to an insistence on the part of the modern that art be considered apart from the problem of life and society in general: he wants art to be absolutely free and unfettered by social and moral considerations. However, those who perceive life to be a unity of many things, each assuming its share in the promotion of the spiritual and physical welfare of society, reject these selfish views of the radical modernist as antisocial, even anti-life.

Aside from these considerations two other factors must be noted which contribute to the problem, and they are largely educational. The earliest training of children is unquestionably along moral lines. Children are told early that some things are nice, proper, desirable, and others ugly, nasty, sinful. In addition, we have to acknowledge that the first art studied in school is literature, not, however, so much for its form as for its content,—the story as such.

It is inevitable that by the time a young person takes up some other art—painting, sculpture, architecture—he has such strong predilections for moralizing content values that the element of beauty expressed in formal values receives scant recognition. This condition has developed a resentment among artists, who hope to combat it by an extreme demonstration of their belief that beauty inherently is independent of the subject used as a vehicle. While this is true in an abstract sense, the fact is undeniable that if art is an expression of life, it must always be influenced by social and ethical conventions.

CLIFF DWELLERS

By George W. Bellows. (Los Angeles Museum of History, Science, and Art)

It is not unlikely that our ideas of the aims of art and of the meaning of beauty may change within the next few decades.

Reinach reassuringly closes his well-known "Apollo" with these speculative remarks: "The art of the twentieth century will be, I am convinced, idealistic and poetical, as well as popular. It will translate the eternal aspiration of man toward that which is lacking in daily life."

VII

THE FANTASTIC; THE GROTESQUE; CARICATURE

The fantastic, even the grotesque, are not uncommon elements in our world, and on that account they are readily recognizable in many works of art. We shall endeavor to make clear, however, that they are to be adjudged to belong to art only when they possess qualities of external beauty, and that many objects fantastic in origin are often lacking in external beauty. Mere extravagant boldness of ideas and forms may only swing away from the real or normal, without giving any definite æsthetic pleasure.

Doubtless in some instances it is the craving for unusual ideas expressed in unusual forms which is the cause of the occurrence of the fantastic and the grotesque, whether or not it succeeds in achieving artistic qualities. On the other hand, the extraordinary, the fanciful, the fantastic, the bizarre, are not uncommon attributes in many arts, and in fact no art, it may be averred, is entirely devoid of these elements; indeed, they give to art one of its most fascinating qualities. The fundamental reason for the use of the fantastic and its exaggerated forms—the grotesque and the bizarre—is undeniably the laudable attempt to give æsthetic pleasure by ingenious means. Confronted with the increasing difficulty of developing new motives in many arts, the ambitious artist, no doubt, is hard put to it to be original, and the imagination is likely to furnish an increasing impetus for original ideas and forms in the realm of art.

Since the dawn of history the craving for the unusual, the extravagant, has manifested itself in the affairs of men. In the history of architecture we all know of the leaning towers of Pisa and Bologna; in clothing, among many other extravagances, we recollect medieval shoes resembling the bills of birds, and the Elizabethan sugar-loaf hat. Again, we cannot ignore that very ancient and striking custom of tattooing, sometimes practiced among primitive tribes with considerable feeling for design, and in the case of the modern sailor and the "sport" with very questionable artistic results. Many a thoughtless individual, permanently and conspicuously disfigured in his youth by ugly tattoo marks, has suffered from his folly after the realization of the social consequences of such inartistic and irremediable pictures has dawned upon him.

The fantastic, in the shape of eccentric perversions, has at times even reached the point of the monstrous, the bestial. In art and literature we have evidences of the fascination of the grotesque element in physical torture and punishment. This is exemplified in the paintings of scenes of religious persecution, preserved in many museums of art. If such works today seem incomprehensible to most of us, we can well afford here to pause and reflect upon the grotesque and bizarre rites which, if we believe published accounts, sometimes develop to the point of cruelty, as practiced by Americans, young and old, in the initiations into clubs, fraternities, and lodges.

Grotesquery of a much more harmless kind is exemplified in many other ways by many fraternal organizations. Many of their public ceremonials are made most spectacular by every manner of grotesque formality, carried out by gaudily uniformed drum majors, marshals, and drill officers leading a great variety of exercises and maneuvers. However, the æsthetic element here is not always present.

Another evidence of the fondness for the fanciful in harmless form may be found in the prevalent use of extraordinary names, both in spelling and in meaning. The modern freedom of choice in that direction tempts undiscerning individuals to flights of fancy. An attempt at the grotesque in designation may be readily traced in the names of Pullman cars, race horses, temporary dwellings, and in every circumstance where it is thought necessary to attract attention by extraordinary means.

DANCING FAUN

Naples Museum

This attempt at the fanciful undeniably exists in many aspects,—in fact, it is basic in human nature; and since it has also historical background, it is unreasonable to expect modern civilization to be free from it, particularly in view of the fact that in the world of art it has become increasingly difficult to be original. Every artist aims to avoid mere repetition of hackneyed ideas and forms. The fantastic, therefore, as distinct from the usual, has a definite, well-founded reason for its existence. We should not feel alarmed, therefore, over the spasmodic occurrence of the grotesque, for it is not likely to supplant the more elevated qualities in art. And used appropriately, as we have stated, fantasy is an absolutely legitimate and desirable element, in that it furnishes innumerable pleasurable forms and ideas which we all realize do not exist anywhere but in the mind of the artist.

In gardens and parks we are sometimes confronted with expressions of the grotesque, that here strive to create pleasing effects, without always succeeding. Strange fountainheads of imaginary design; arbors made of twisted, knotty branches, often suggesting animal forms; decorations of all sorts composed of shells, colored bottles, fragments of various things such as pebbles or colored stones,—all these features are put to use with variable results. Seaside resorts and summer dwellings furnish many illustrations of the grotesque: in the arches made of the jawbones of whales, in chairs, tables, and other so-called pieces of furniture made from sections of the vertebræ and the whale's skeleton. Shrubs and trees, particularly in Europe, not infrequently are trained and clipped into fantastic forms in the practice of topiary art. At times distinctly beautiful effects have been produced by using architectural forms, while naturalistic imitations of animal forms seem unconvincing and inappropriate. This old and quaint custom, however, owing to the cost of labor, enjoys less vogue in recent years.

Indoors, also, those of little æsthetic training at times yield to the craving for the fantastic, the grotesque, and the bizarre in the hope of achieving an artistic ensemble. Here furniture and bric-a-brac in very exaggerated cases of absolute lack of artistic sensibilities yield a rich harvest of offensive objects; and when this is the case, the front parlor may be referred to as a storehouse of questionable works of art.

In some few homes still the shrine for so-called objects of art is the parlor. One is moved to ask why everything in the parlor is regarded as so artistic, because often its contents are so incapable of practical use. Gold chairs one cannot sit on comfortably; vases one cannot put flowers into, because they are likely to tip over when filled with water; chandeliers obscured with superfluous ornament; pillows bead-embroidered with the likenesses of Indian chiefs or replicas of the California missions, painful to the unwary head that rests against them,—such are, frequently, favored parlor ornaments. Here also, in the parlor, may be found the footstool shaped to represent a curled-up cat or dog—a heritage of past generations—and the dedication chair constructed from the horns of cattle or deer. It is impossible not to speak of these things if we are serious in our purpose to make these discussions of practical value. Fortunately, our present age has largely outgrown such monstrosities, and they are not likely to become popular again unless we should suffer a serious lapse in our taste. It is not surprising that the owners of such things were content to sacrifice the front parlor to meaningless conventionality so long as they were permitted to enjoy life in other, more appropriately furnished, parts of the house. We cannot close our eyes to the fact that parlors still are dedicated to a pseudo-art which is merely grotesque and useless. Some of the most distressing expressions of bad taste of recent date that come to one's mind are shiny brass inkwells representing the heads of kings, emperors, and presidents, the top of the craniums having been sliced off and put on hinges, to permit the inside to hold the ink. There are actual cases where the hair on the top of the head has been replaced by real bristles, to serve as a pen-cleaner and as a tribute to a no-less-popular idol than Roosevelt. This instance perhaps represents the most striking absence of a sense of fitness and good taste. But what argument can be made for the small-scale replicas of campaniles, towers, shafts, four or five inches high, with a thermometer or a clock fastened to the front?

There are in Europe several museums where the directors, conscious of the importance of the problem created by such articles, have collected a whole roomful of such inartistic things, with the idea of discouraging, by the weight of evidence, further spread of such "objects of art." These collections of "horrible examples," however, at first threatened to fail in their educational mission; in fact, for a time, when public taste was at rather a low ebb, they were misunderstood, many people being greatly attracted to them when a glimpse through the door had indicated the character of the exhibits. In spite of the partial failure of this European educational undertaking, it is to be hoped that every public museum in this country will devote some space to exhibits of this sort, to counteract the deplorable use of energy and good material in the prospective manufacture of inartistic novelties, souvenirs, mementos, and all the many things people are tempted to purchase for want of an understanding of what is really artistically worth while. Booths on amusement piers, shops at tourist hotels, and even so-called art stores are undoubtedly still reaping a seasonal harvest from people with no appreciation of the significance of such articles. Fortunately, many inartistic bizarre things are only short-lived. They are discarded on more mature reflection, and disappear in the natural reassertion of true art principles. The serious student of art should not lessen his standards by yielding to the peculiar fascination of the ugly article just because it is different.

In architecture, on account of its more permanent form, it is more difficult to free the world from inartistic bizarre expression. The very widely known family tomb of the Sagrada family in Barcelona, erected at very great cost in the form of a church, with its meaningless, grotesque, French-pastry ornament, will offend generations.

But, after all, the gargoyles on the Cathedral of Notre Dame in Paris, while they are fantastic, grotesque, and bizarre, are, nevertheless, genuinely artistic. Moreover, they are useful in carrying water away from the building. The well-known Notre Dame gargoyles permit us to make the point which will enable us definitely to arrive at a basis for a fair appreciation of things of the grotesque order. The grotesque has undoubtedly a merited place in art, provided it has artistic qualities. We are here again obliged to emphasize the fact that the fundamental qualities of fitness to use, soundness of structure, good proportion, rhythmic line, harmony, are applicable here, as in anything we properly call art. It does not matter how grotesque the idea may be, if it is put into a convincing, agreeable art form it undoubtedly has its place.

It is easy to be confused in dealing with this problem. We all know that semiclassic figure, by Giovanni da Bologna, of Mercury, caduceus in his left hand, his right arm outstretched, sailing into space from a pedestal. As a piece of decorative sculpture it has few equals. This charming figure has many times been turned into a lighting-fixture in which a cluster of lights of considerable weight has been fastened to the outstretched right arm. The effect of this unfortunate combination is painful to the eye on account of the complete destruction of its suggestion of balance so beautifully calculated in the original. The only criterion, then, that we have in all such problems of artistic judgment, whether in pictorial art, in sculpture, architecture, music, literature, drama, the dance, decoration, furniture, or in gardening, is simply this, Is the formal manner of expression æsthetically satisfactory or is it not? There are numerous evidences in all the arts that real artistic achievement is possible in the realm of the grotesque and bizarre as long as the fundamental laws of beauty are observed.

The artistic achievement of the grotesque dates back to the time of the Assyrians and Egyptians, with their curious combination of winged creatures such as the winged bull, the sphinx, and the great variety of Asiatic deities possessed of physical characteristics no human being possesses. What extraordinary wealth of fantastic imagination confronts us also in the art of the Western world, in the centaurs, satyrs, nymphs, sprites, gnomes, witches, goblins, and other fabulous beings—all the children of a fantastic imagination—so often artistically expressed! Even the Christian religion has not been able to function without devils and angels of great multiplicity of form. In America, where Chinese civilization has been made familiar in many localities in processions and rituals, we have learned to recognize the dragon as one of the most fantastic expressions of Oriental imagination.

Again, the characters in the literature of Æsop, Greek theatrical masks, the baroque in architecture, the rococo motifs, centaurs in the art of the modern Von Stuck and Böcklin, the music of Wagner, the drawings of Aubrey Beardsley, Japanese tea gardens,—all these indicate different expressions of grotesque ideas and forms in æsthetically satisfactory ways.

Many times, particularly in Gothic architecture, the term "grotesque" conveys the idea of humorous distortion or exaggeration, where it is simply "grotto-esque." The term literally applied refers to the style of art found in the grottoes or baths of the ancients. It came into being toward the end of the fifteenth century, when archæological researches brought to light the fantastic, often humorous, decorations of the private apartments of the Romans. The word since then, as applied to such creations, has acquired common currency, and it has spread to everything which provokes a smile by a real or pretended violation of the laws of nature.

Humor has the same meaning for every age and every race. Doubtless earliest man enjoyed his laugh practically in the same way as the modern. Except for the Assyrians, humor has been a quality in every age, in every race. The Assyrians, it is true, furnished no grounds for crediting them with a sense of humor. The amount of fun one gets out of Assyrian relics is very small indeed. But the Greeks came very near to what we consider the comic; in fact, they had something better than jocoseness, and that was joyousness. The Romans eventually developed humor of a somewhat coarse type; and humor, expressed in the "grotto-esque," as we have seen, has had a prominent place in literature and art ever since.

The sense of humor fortunately has grown with the centuries, and with us it has become a very important element in life and in art. The political cartoon, the comic supplement of our press, and the moving pictures are furnishing convincing testimony to the modern demand for the whimsical and comical, and for the caricature—its graphic expression. Freedom of speech, common sense, and the much-cherished idea of equality have permitted us to indulge in laughter at the expense of everyone,—and, fortunately, of ourselves as well,—without regard for wealth, power, and privilege. In fact, one of the most popular pastimes of the American humorist in word or pencil is constantly to remind those in power that we are all made of the same clay. Mark Twain in literature typifies our natural power and appreciation of humor. No country has produced a humorist who achieved such universal acclaim as the author of "Innocents Abroad." On the stage we have developed many popular figures who excel in subtle humorous qualities which are likely to be overlooked by superficial observers. There are, at times, passages in popular comic performances on the motion-picture screen which in all fairness must be recognized as gems of grotesque acting. In caricature the popular daily cartoon, with its often high standards of form and draftsmanship, has added much to the joy of living, in its humorous exploitation of the perplexities, the various absurdities, of the human family.

What the burlesque, the parody, and the travesty are to literature, the caricature is to graphic art. The caricature as a playful, grotesque exaggeration of striking features of peculiarities is one of the best means in humanization and democratization, and in performing that function has become a widely cultivated art. In emphasizing the salient features of any subject, the process of caricature is closely allied to the method of idealization. While idealization is commonly thought to enlarge and emphasize all that is desirable but not really true, the caricature accentuates what is true but not commonly accepted as desirable. The ideal and the caricature both begin with the normal. They develop, however, in opposite directions. A portrait conceived in the spirit of the caricature is likely to be more interesting and significant than a portrait of the idealistic type. Perhaps in times of stress, caricature, the parody, the travesty, have taken an unkind advantage of the physical and mental imperfections of humanity. If they at times seem to go too far in this direction, they compensate, on the other hand, by reminding us of the dangers of false ideals, bad habits, and selfishness.

It is not unusual, indeed it is in accord with tradition, to give to caricature a very low position in the world of art. The low rating given to it, many feel, is an injustice. The artistic, the truly humorous caricature certainly has the most intimate connection in our day with life. It follows every change, every tendency; and its leading representatives are always with the progressive element. They are, in fact, the bold outposts in that old struggle of art with life. Furthermore, they open up, as much as any art, new avenues of æsthetic enjoyment. The caricature deserves recognition because of the very manner of its unusual appeal. It is one of the effective factors in a general education toward the enjoyment of art and life.

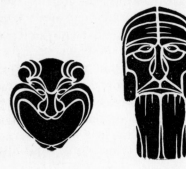

VIII

THE CONTENT IN ART—THE SUBJECT REVIEWED
HISTORICALLY

We have emphasized in the preceding chapters why the idealistic concept in art is regarded by many as superior to the realistic; so now we shall trace the entire scale of values, thus arrived at, directly in terms of the subject as it presents itself in the kaleidoscope of the history of art. We shall have no difficulty in realizing that in every national unit giving rise to a great and significant art the subject matter has been largely determined by religious, ethical, social, political, and economic factors, all serving at different times as the vehicle to express beauty.

We find, first of all, that the sublime expressed in terms of religious symbols holds a foremost position in the scale of subject values. Approximating it in importance come, in keeping with the aristocratic idea, the God-chosen representatives of divine creation, such as czars, emperors, and Cæsars of every brand. All that which seems socially worth coveting for the average human has always been regarded as giving greater importance to a work of art than the undesirable. The work of art representing a condition of affluence is rated higher than one suggesting a milieu of poverty. Although, with the spread of democracy and the gradual abolition of inherited privilege, we in America are less moved by class prejudices, the social importance of the subject, by reason of historical bias and through association of ideas, continues to be a potent influence in the evaluation of works of art. Anything symbolizing power, or superiority in a social sense, is likely to warp the layman's mind as to the real meaning of a work of art. And this complexity of content values persists as a problem all by itself, independent of the problem of formal beauty.

Physical power is no less impressive delineated in art than it is in reality; indeed, the entire scale of human attributes, physical and spiritual, as pointed out before, is a well-recognized basis of appeal in subject matter. A statue of a Hercules impresses the man on the street more than a statue of a man deficient in physical prowess, even when the latter may have more significance as a work of art.

Whenever academic tradition governs the world of art, prescribed and arbitrary rules give each subject its place of importance. Aside from these considerations, the layman often ingenuously believes that the larger a picture the greater its importance; similarly, to him a picture dealing with many figures is worthy of more praise than a single portrait; and a full-length piece commands more respect than a mere bust portrait. In his eyes some subjects, particularly landscapes, have no claim to special distinction other than to serve as a background for more important figural subjects. What condescension there is in the oft-made remark "He is only a landscape painter"! And what of the painter of the lowly still life? If people had any idea of beauty per se, so many fine still-life paintings would not go unnoticed.

Ruskin, in keeping with the spirit of his time, had a marked predilection for "noble" subjects, and his scorn for the ignoble, irrespective of its beauty, cannot be denied of having added its weight to the prejudices of his time. If he had consistently exercised his so often and convincingly demonstrated feeling for beauty, his impetuous denunciation of Whistler's humble but beautiful nocturnes could not have involved him in the embarrassing situation caused by Whistler's law suit.

Our review of values with respect to content in art should have made clear the following conclusion: a work of art may deal with any object in an æsthetically pleasing way. Therefore we cannot very well place any trust in the oft-asserted contention that what is considered of artistic significance to-

day was not so regarded in days gone by. Indeed, if we did,
we should deprive ourselves of the most engaging pleasure that

ADORATION OF THE MAGI
By Ghirlandajo. (Florentine Academy)

art offers; namely, its multiformity of expression. While the
choice of subject matter in art throughout succeeding periods
must justly seem most vacillating, it is worth repeating that
the same abstract qualities of beauty in the sense of formal

relations have endured at all times. There are many types in which beauty may be expressed; but beauty itself is immutable. The subject matter in art may naturally have reflected the changing conditions of the ages; whatever constitutes artistic appeal in methods of representation will be found a universal quality throughout all periods. Formal elements of beauty in a work of art—those which are dependent upon line and form, balance, harmony, rhythm, color, technique, composition, and arrangement—have changed but little, if viewed in the light of art history. A good design has always been recognized as a good design.

However, the use of different subjects in art, as they appeal to our intellect by reason of their moral, religious, political, and sentimental character, has, on the other hand, shown very many variations. To many people only those pictures are acceptable which depict the habits, morals, and customs of bygone days and periods. Undoubtedly it is the *genre* picture that particularly controls and fastens the interest of the layman upon art, and for that reason its psychology cannot be underestimated. It will be found that the genuineness, the veracity of atmosphere, in a picture is very intimately connected with this power of appeal. The true artists of any period convincingly and intentionally reflected the *milieu* of their days; on the other hand, many historical pictures lacking in conviction seem uninteresting and affected. The pictures which at once become engaging to the mind are those which spring from the personal experience of the artist, irrespective of their technical language. Fresh and candid pictorial documents belonging to any period never fail to charm us in their perennial power of appeal. The subjects represented may in their appearance differ vastly; but the spirit of suggested realism, of vital interpretation, has ever been the same in the masterworks of both new and old schools.

It is a fixed habit with many people to evaluate paintings according to their so-called moral power, as expressed by the subject,—as if the subject as such had any part in this ques-

MATERNITY

By Gari Melchers. (Corcoran Gallery of Art, Washington, D. C.)

tion of moral uplift; as if representative art could exert the direct moral appeal of the preacher. The fact that we can have the artistically good religious picture, on the one hand, and the artistically bad religious picture, on the other, will prove the fallacy of this very common idea. It is undeniable that the loftiness of style, the linear charm, the stately balance, of a Bellini Madonna stir our instinctive feelings of exaltation just as much as the expression of maternal pride and devotion in her face; for superb qualities of content and form here work harmoniously toward unity of expression. On the other hand, to one æsthetically sensitive, a treatment of the same subject, even that of the Madonna, that is crude and vulgar in form and color can only be conducive to dissatisfaction rather than elevation of mind. The common confidence which exists in the emotional and spiritual effect of a subject, independent of the abstract in artistic quality inherent in the manner of representation, is not always based on any careful analysis of all factors but is merely the result of prejudice and confusion of ideas.

It was undoubtedly a historical coincidence that the first important easel pictures painted were of a religious character. The Church, being the moving spirit in every human activity, during the fifteenth century constituted itself the first real art patron, with the result that the motives of the earliest important pictures were all of an ecclesiastical trend. It would be very misleading to conclude, just because that was the case and because they seem so abundant in this period, that all religious pictures are necessarily of a superior order. Since the epoch of the Madonna and Child is undoubtedly that of many of the world's great masterpieces, the popular prejudice in favor of all such subjects in art is easily understood. The fact that the early age of easel painting, that of the Renaissance, has never been equaled or surpassed in loftiness of style, imaginative fancy, and disciplined technique very easily explains the high esteem in which it is held.

If in judging any painting its force of appeal to our sentiment is acknowledged, the abstract formal relations of the canvas should at once be taken into account. If they are found to be of equal import with the inner meaning, all is well. But how few preserve this discriminating attitude in their judgments!

To many laymen unable to comprehend beauty of form it seldom occurs that a religious picture may be bad. Every religious picture is likely to be treated with great reverence, as if in its very nature it must be good art. The idea that it may be bad is perhaps even regarded as sacrilegious, no matter how distressingly composed, no matter how stupid in technique, the picture of the Madonna and Child may be. Very considerable numbers of ugly religious paintings, by copyists and imitators of Raphael, Murillo, and other good painters, brought over during the early days of Spanish colonization, may be found in America. The conventional idea of respect for everything religious has removed these pictures almost entirely from the sphere of criticism, even though many are æsthetically distinctly unsatisfactory. That the goodness of a picture may manifest itself in two ways,—in the intelligent expression of the idea, and in the qualities of abstract beauty as well,—this alone should be the foundation of artistic criticism.

What is true in a special way of the religious picture is even more true in general of the so-called old masters. The term "old master" is properly restricted to an old painting which is supremely good and equally valuable. But every old canvas, showing in divers ways the ravages of time, is likely to be termed an old master. That it might be the work of an old-time inexperienced apprentice or journeyman painter of little ability seldom enters into the problem. There have been inferior artists at all times. The many remote places which occasionally give up a heretofore unknown painting of supposedly great beauty and enormous value have rarely contributed to the discovery of pictures which would justify their being taken from their hiding-places. Many speculative minds are unduly fascinated by the possibility of the discovery of a so-called old master. As if there were really a likelihood that many are still to be discovered! Most paintings worthy of any recognition are duly known, authenticated, and recorded. But the merry chase goes on, like the perennial search for buried treasure on the palm-studded islands of the Pacific.

The fact remains that the religious picture, whether painted by an old master or a modern master, is a great favorite in the public museum. Because of the general disregard for technical values, the final judgment is rarely based upon the qualities inherent in formal excellence.

While so many of the great pictures of the masters of the Renaissance were religious in motif, with the lessening of the influence of the Church and with the waning of patronage by a rich aristocracy the subject character of pictures naturally changed, and other motifs than the Saints or Madonna and Child were cultivated. However, the representation on canvas, and in wood or marble, of the Christ Child and Mother, expressing the glorification of the joy and tragedy of motherhood, has occupied artists of all times, even those of our own. American artists like George de Forest Brush, Abbott Thayer, Gari Melchers, and Paul Manship have treated this subject with great sympathy and convincing feeling. During the seventeenth century,—the greatest period of painting in Spain,—although religious pictures were incidentally continued, the portrait of the leading citizen and the nobleman, and the battle picture, began to come to the fore, and also the realistic subject of everyday occurrence.

Since any art period, particularly that of a realistic trend, reflects the political, religious, and economic history of its time, art has often supplied a truthful background invaluable for the historian. Thus to the serious student art becomes doubly interesting, while the person merely looking for passing pleasures in art often dismisses period pictures as merely amusing, forgetting how we ourselves might appear if pictorially represented to some future gallery-stroller a hundred years hence. For example, the last twenty years here and abroad surely have been as sensational with respect to fashion in dress as anything we may meet in the early Spanish, French, or Dutch pictures. Velásquez's "Meniñas," with their odd and cumbersome hoop skirts, are assuredly no more amusing than the early-twentieth-century ladies in their hobble skirts and carriage-wheel hats.

The northern countries gradually turned to other than religious subjects, and their artists addressed their talents to the exploitation—with a realism sometimes very frank—of subject matter which is often shocking to many people of moral prejudices. In spite of the realistic delineation of everyday occurrences in the art of the seventeenth-century Dutch, their art as an expression of formal beauty was on a par with the best of the world. These Dutch painters—Ter Borch, Vermeer of Delft, Metsu—knew how to impart to their work a charm of beauty of design, a feeling of conviction, which will insure to any painting a permanent place in the history of art. Pictures like theirs, whenever they possess a quality of beauty in line and form and color, are not inferior works of art. The Dutch painters, with their humble subjects, sometimes of restricted size, certainly prove this very forcibly.

The veracious art of the sturdy Dutch finds its antithesis in the ultrarefined idealistic art of the English portrait-painter, like that of Gainsborough, Reynolds, Romney, or Hoppner. Whereas the Dutch painters portrayed invariably the true physical aspects of things, the English aimed at an idealized spiritual representation of their aristocracy and upper classes. Although we admire the stately dignity of the English school, it assuredly does not give us much of an insight into the life of the English people. If art presents to us a cross section of life, their art barely scratched the surface of their social structure. Hogarth practically stands out alone as the cool observer, the sometimes mordant cynic, among the painters of England, showing in bold ruthlessness indecencies, corrupt politics, and decadent life of some of his contemporaries. Hogarth's position as an individualistic analyzer of his time foreshadows the even more personal outlook and realism expressed in such of our modern American artists as Bellows. In the long run Hogarth as a figure will retain the admiration of the world, not only for the manner of his painting but also for his broad and illuminating conception of his professional responsibilities. The public frequently points at the constant change in the subject as a proof that art is simply a matter of choice. But to take a subject and interpret it convincingly in its proper environment is worthy of the artist's best efforts. There is hardly a greater step than from the realistic Dutch painter to the idealistic English portrait-painter; although we know that the two are intimately connected by the art of Van Dyck, who laid the foundation for the great English eighteenth-century school and, in his more polished and restrained art, bridged the gap between the sensuous realism of Rubens and the refined portraits of Gainsborough and Reynolds.

It is natural that the ideal—if it *is* an ideal—of physical beauty painted by the Dutch is scarcely sympathetic to anybody outside of the Dutch nation. Their resistance to the southern tradition in æsthetics, as well as to any attempt from the south to interfere with their political existence, culminated in a spirit of independence that is well-nigh amazing. They could neither be seduced by the exotic nor forced by arms to be anybody but themselves. The æsthetic ideal of the Dutch was homemade. However, the average American traveling abroad for the first time is severely shaken in his belief in the superiority of European masters when he sees the pictures by Rubens or Jordaens in the museums of France, England, Holland, and Germany. Their frank realism is repugnant to him at first sight, though eventually he learns to admire their skill and technique, their joyful exuberance, and their big, decorative style. The Dutch of these days are absolutely by themselves in the outspoken realism of their art. This realism is simply the reflection of the life of these people, whose very manner and whose language were and still are free from prudishness and false modesty. Van Dyck carried over into England, his adopted country, all the technical brilliancy of his great teacher Rubens; and in the works of Gainsborough, Reynolds,

INTERIOR, WITH WOMAN AND BOY
By De Hooch. (Courtesy of Wallace Collection)

Hoppner, and others this brilliancy grows into the stately and somewhat less temperamental dignity of a calm and more stoic race.

The difference in subject matter between the typical expressions of art of the Dutch and of the English may seem radical;

but it is not any more radical than the difference between the two of them, on the one hand, and, on the other, the Watteaus, Fragonards, and Bouchers of the eighteenth-century French. While art in England portrayed idealistically many people of high social position, and was always careful to leave a good moral impression for the future historian, the French painter of the eighteenth century cared naught for the deluge to come after him. French painters, like their royal patrons, snapped their fingers in the face of future historians, and in representations of subjects disclosing lax morals surpassed even the sometimes coarse realism of the Dutch. While the Dutch painter dwells upon the moral light-heartedness of his people by using as models these same people in their everyday surroundings, the French painter puts wings on his aristocratic patrons, so to speak, and transfers them into an Arcadia animated with angels and other mythological beings endowed with special privileges.

This merely illustrates another phase of the change of the subject ideal,—an ideal that will never remain the same, but will always vary with the political, social, and moral background of a people. So long as the art expression of a people is in harmony with some characteristic phase of their life, there will never be a lack of genuine interest in it. It is only when the art of one country is transplanted into another country of different inheritance that bad art is likely to be the result. The craving for the foreign and the affectation of an ideal based on alien backgrounds have diverted the attention of many good painters from the fields of inspiration in their immediate surroundings. The cloudy mirroring of their own civilization and environment was the inevitable result of their shortsightedness and lack of real interest in their work. Thus in our own country this delayed the rise of a native school of art by half a century or more.

Today we may observe the modern Filipino affecting the art of the Paris atelier as the national art of his own country. He is not convincing in his pretentious canvases; the artistic

HARLEQUIN AND COLUMBINE

By Watteau. (Courtesy of Wallace Collection)

ingenuity of the Filipino is seen to much better advantage in
his native craftsmanship, applied to utilitarian objects. The
efforts of many technically well-equipped modern painters to

revive in their art the civilization of bygone days is always singularly disappointing. The classicizing and fragile art of an Alma Tadema can hardly be called a genuine contribution to the art of our day, in spite of its beauty of design. That the Greeks had few easel painters, in the modern sense, is doubtless regrettable; but we get through the channels of literature and sculpture all we ever can hope to know about their lives, manners, and civilization, and the pleasant generalization upon Greek life of such a modern painter as Alma Tadema does not add anything to our knowledge of the Greeks derived from other sources. The beginning of decay in any period of art has always been foreshadowed by the imitation of the methods and subjects of bygone periods and of other peoples; and art, therefore, is never more interesting and wholesome than when it has been concerned exclusively with the restricted atmosphere in which the artist belongs by nature or race. Greek art, the Renaissance, the art of modern France, of Sweden, and even of America, will illustrate this contention. The great art of any people has come out of the logical development of their particular civilization. The reactionary methods of the nineteenth-century painters had to lead inevitably to a revolt, the full weight of which we were made to feel in the impressionist of the seventies and, right now, in the experiments of our postimpressionists.

What today constitutes the subject ideal is hard to say. We are living in an age of experimentation, even of turmoil, and an adjustment to a definite concept is not yet in sight. There are today certain older, conservative members of the professions who think any academically inherited subject is sufficient to their needs as long as it is academically approved. They are comparable to any of the older generation of painters of any period, who were similarly governed by school precepts. They hesitate to concern themselves with the materials afforded by their own environment. To this reactionary class belong many of our popular painters, who often borrow their subjects from history books rather than rely upon their own experiences. On the other hand, as an extreme in the opposite direction, we have the members of the artistic professions who for many

PORTRAIT OF MRS. POLK

By Sir Joshua Reynolds. (Museum of Fine Arts, Boston)

reasons rebel against the academic. The really earnest ones have graduated from the conventional academic schools, sometimes with conspicuous honors. They eventually, like Cézanne, by slow degrees have become dissatisfied with the monotony and hopelessness of repeated performances, and, led by perfectly honest motives, they begin to experiment, with no idea of reward of any kind other than to gratify a desire for research. Often they make great sacrifices in their search for a new expression of their ideas, go into seclusion as a proof of their seriousness—and work! Although these latest efforts, because of their marked divergence from the traditional, have attracted wide attention, the public, in the light of traditional art concepts, finds itself quite unable to appreciate them. Despite solemn warnings from the historically informed that similar crises have occurred before, and that doubt has turned into approval, this time no such warning has any effect. The sympathetic critic in vain cites examples of other great innovators,—Constable's pathetic experience in 1825, the Barbizon men in general, and particularly the great French impressionists of the seventies,—Monet, Manet, Renoir, Pissarro,—who insisted upon the painting of effects rather than facts. But to no avail: the public in general declines to take our latest experimenters seriously. While in the case of former innovations only things visible were involved, some of our recent art,—that is, the futurist,—professes to have invaded the realm of the psychic; that is to say, claims that painting, to the artist, has suddenly ceased to be a method for objective expression and has turned, through symbols known only to him, to the giving of visual form to his subjective emotion. He no longer finds it either necessary or useful to paint objects for their own sake and so to have his subjective feelings subordinated. The rabid negation of the traditional has never assumed such outspoken form as in certain instances today. It has become, as we have seen, very largely a direct contest between the objective idealist and the subjective realist.

What has become known in modern art as cubism is, if we understand the cubist, no novelty to any artist of academic training and precepts. The novelty merely consists in presenting to the public a principle in graphic form as a finished thing which was formerly looked upon as a basic constructive start. From Egyptian and Assyrian days to the present we find the cubistic principle of representation in planes in drawing and also in painting and sculpture. It cannot be denied that it is a perfectly sound principle, a fundamental idea which no serious artist could ever afford to neglect. To see and represent things geometrically in planes is the most primitive method of representation, and most economical and interesting at the same time. Japanese wood-carvings of centuries ago, many of the masterpieces of the Italian primitives, and modern wood toys are as typical of the cubistic idea as the modern paintings which attempt representation in the same fashion. The cubistic idea in emphasizing volume is æsthetically sound, and is nothing but a healthy expression of the protest of certain conscientious men in the profession against a growing insipid and loose construction in works of art. Cubism is inherent in the structural element in any good painting, whether of old or new schools. However, to make it the sole feature of a picture, to the exclusion of any other quality, is obviously questionable to any person trained in the belief that the constructive features of a picture must be modified by decorative aspects. A building left in the raw, so to speak,—merely in steel construction,—is artistic, sometimes, if the engineer happens to feel toward his material as does an artist; although for purposes of refinement it is meant to be eventually clothed by the varied and modified forms of the architect. Sometimes steel construction alone is not at all uninteresting in its decorative aspects, and occasionally this fact is acknowledged by the architect when he allows himself the unconventional thing in not covering up the engineer's work with traditional architectural forms. But in general, in any work of art, the structural foundation, important as this is, cannot adequately express the character of an object. The structural idea will always assert itself unless art ceases to exist, and the fact that it has been expressed so vigorously by the cubists proves merely their resentment against the meaningless representation of trivial things, particularly those of the "pretty-pretty," or saccharine, variety. Closely associated with the constructive cubism of many modern artists we observe a fondness for strength in color as well as in form. It is in keeping with the philosophy of the cubist in eliminating all characterless middle values in the modeling of his material, and it is absolutely consistent with the idea of simplicity that underlies the theory. The best works of cubism are

THE BROKEN OAK

From a water color by Francis McComas. The marked structural emphasis reveals forms in geometric planes—a sound demonstration of the cubistic idea. The technical treatment is bold to a degree unusual in water color

excellent in action and in decorative pattern. This in some instances is not denied by the most reactionary. The cubist, then, is really not outside the pale of the academic; he does not refuse to use sound conventional art principles, such as rhythm, harmony, and balance, which play so very important a part in academic work. Many modern landscapes and works of sculpture of cubistic tendencies will find a permanent place in the history of art, and it is already evident that the effect of the movement has been beneficial to art. Let us try to realize, for a moment, what the outcome would have been if cubism had not been revived for us at this time in such vigorous language. The complacency and self-satisfaction of great numbers of academic painters would have remained unchallenged, and by this time would have arrived at a point where it could only be called uninteresting and lifeless. The vigorous spirit of the cubists, their contagious method of plastic thinking and expression, have given new impetus to art. Whenever it succeeds, if we view their work without preconceived prejudice, their art is decidedly decorative, reverting as it does to the old, original idea of the true function of painting; and this achievement should be greeted with approval. In substance, cubism as a principle has always been a means toward an end, and it is only recently that it has been emphasized as an end in itself.

Many do not feel equally reassured in the case of other post-impressionistic tendencies, such as futurism. Apparently the futurist is trying to express his psychic complex in graphic terms. To most people unable to grasp his symbols he is obscure not so much in his verbally stated creed as in his attainments. We ought at any rate to respect his attempts, although we have perhaps no understanding of the result. However, to many it is doubtful whether psychic emotion can be represented by pictorial formulas. The Düsseldorf painter, with his excessive fondness for literary subjects, was no less guilty of trespassing than the futurist, with his vagaries which might perhaps be more convincingly expressed by literature or music. But this point remains an open question, and we can well afford to wait, since the great majority of painters have decided not to go beyond the limitations established by the experiments of the impressionist, who has by this time been accepted by the academies. The average art student will find so much of interest in the traditional aspects of art that he need not feel disturbed at the sporadic symptoms of æsthetic research workers.

IX

REPRESENTATION VERSUS DECORATION

In the vast field of literature on art, as well as in the spirited discussions of artists, we meet with two pleas not uncommonly presented in sharp contradistinction. One is to the effect that the aim of the arts is solely representation of appearances. In so many words, some writers have stated that decoration is not art. The believers in this limitation of the function of art have always found adherents. However, we must not forget that there are other equally sincere and successful groups of art workers who, conversely, hold to their conviction that the mere expression of an idea through recognizable symbols devoid of artistic qualities is not worthy of being called art, and they cultivate, in addition, the element called decoration. Although the thoughtful student will recognize at once in the subject of this chapter a fundamental idea presented in disguise,—that is to say, Is art merely imitation?—the importance of the problem as expressed in the existing conflicting views warrants us in once more emphasizing and presenting the problem from a different angle. We shall therefore give the advocates for either side an opportunity to plead their cases; but after that we must allow the student of art to settle the matter with his own æsthetic conscience.

Representation, as such, does not create beauty in the fullest sense. (This, to be sure, we tried to determine previously.) Only when the object represented has been treated formally in such a way as to create a beauty which is expressed in abstract terms of rhythmic lines, agreeable interrelation of areas and patterns, effective contrasts, color harmonies, and the many other abstract qualities especially dealt with in later chapters of this book, can we properly speak of the work as art in the complete meaning of the word. The thoughtless insistence upon mere representation invariably leads to unselective imitation. This naturalism—and such it is in formal expression—means essentially the same as naturalism in subject. In either case it signifies that motifs have been used *exactly* as they appear in nature and presented without reference to æsthetic principles. We have already indicated, indeed, that idealism in the academic sense may be expressed in two ways,—either in the choice of subject or in the formal treatment of the subject. And the expression of the form in an ideal is precisely what so many artists aim to achieve in the decorative manner.

Paintings exist in two fundamentally different types,—the mural painting and the easel painting,—each governed by special considerations. The mural painting, particularly that of large proportion, must not destroy the architectural sense of the wall upon which it appears. The wall invariably carries a load, and anything which would weaken the appearance of support it furnishes to the ceiling above must be avoided. If the mural painting respects this requirement imposed upon it by architecture, it may deal with any subject. In addition, a mural painting, owing to its often being placed at a very great distance from the nearest point of observation, must often sacrifice finer chacterization, particularly of emotions.

Easel pictures exist entirely for themselves, separated from the surroundings by the frame; they have no restriction forced upon them by any exigencies of the surroundings in which they are used, since, according to the plan of their creators, they may be transported at will and viewed anywhere. The easel picture has undoubtedly grown out of a demand for increasing opportunities for expression other than those furnished by stationary walls.

It would seem that, largely owing to the lack of a suitable technique, many paintings until the fourteenth century were of a decorative character; that is, they were carried out in tempera or mosaic, to become a part of a wall. In the work of all the early painters we are distinctly conscious that it was executed under certain restrictions. These earlier artists are often spoken of as the primitives. The Byzantines and the early Italians had not yet developed the power of representation as we see it first in Giotto. The complete absence of technical sophistication and a disregard for photographic imitation of appearances are characteristic of the primitives.

THE JOURNEY OF THE MAGI TO BETHLEHEM

This early Italian painting by Benozzo Gozzoli is not only expressive of an idea but also decorative in its treatment. (Palazzo Riccardi, Florence)

The temptation, partly the result of technical improvements and of greater skillfulness, to deceive the eye into perceiving realities was too great to be resisted, and the so-called plastic modeling of objects became increasingly the temptation of painters. It is important to dwell upon this point, because this practice has become an accepted method in the Western world and threatens to destroy the decorative concept of modern

Japanese art. When one considers that painting has one of its most splendid opportunities in the beautification of surfaces by means of color carried by line, form, light, and dark, and that as pure design it does not necessarily support an idea, one cannot help feeling that painting which is practiced on a

THE STRUGGLE FOR EXISTENCE

A story-telling painting much better suited to literary treatment. There is little feeling for formal beauty in this oil painting by Christian Krohg

misconception of this function is lacking in a desirable element. The difficulty to a large extent is inherent in the concession to painting of subjects which are more suitably expressed by literary means,—the story, the anecdote, the romantic in general. The above painting by Krohg is a typical example of this kind; its story touches our heartstrings, but it assuredly has no beauty.

Whatever the reason for this latter type of painting, we are, in view of the existing facts, obliged to recognize two distinct types: the ugly picture and the decorative picture, the beautiful picture. Unbeautiful pictures, often of the story-telling type, however, are regarded by many artists as questionable in principle. The most popular achievements of this type were the *genre* pictures, the anecdotal pictures of the Munich and Düsseldorf school of the late seventies. The subjects used in them could in many cases be more sympathetically rendered by literary means, and to the layman actually do become more enjoyable in the literary works of such men as Dickens. The point to be made clear is that some anecdotal pictures are abstractly beautiful and therefore decorative, others devoid of that desirable quality. There is no sense in excluding the anecdote as a subject in painting, provided in the treatment, manner of its presentation, it gives pleasure not possible in other media. A story told in literary form holds one's interest for human *and* for formal reasons—why should it not be the same in painting?

Such a well-known story-telling picture as Hovenden's "Breaking Home Ties," admired by very large numbers of people at several expositions in the United States, in all its sentimentality, would be much more appealing in literature. It is too "literatesque" a subject to be justifiably used in painting. If you were to turn the painting upside down, and were compelled to forget its story for a moment, it would become uninteresting in the extreme, even appear ugly; it would be chaotic. Although this test may seem somewhat extreme, it is, however, true that if you treat a canvas by Abbey, Brangwyn, or Alexander in the same way, it would still exert a charm, because of a certain beautiful arrangement of spaces, by reason of the relation of these spaces, of coloring, and of design generally, which gives æsthetic interest to the painting, no matter from what distance it is viewed or from what point of view. If this experiment is tried a number of times, it will convince everyone of the reasonableness of the distinction between the unselective imitative, the naturalistic, the unbeautiful, and the decorative, the abstractly beautiful, type of art.

Both types, however, have been emphasized throughout the history of art, but in constantly shifting equilibrium. Sometimes one type has dominated and then the other. In modern times the naturalistic imitative picture has had to yield to the conscious emphasis of form and color we meet in the decorative picture. The aims, then, of these two modes of expression are fundamentally different, and are such a constant source of confusion to the student that a lack of appreciation of the principles involved in one or the other leads to as many arguments as the conflicts between idealism and realism in subject matter. The decorative picture, in its modern revived form, has come to us from the Orient. The Japanese screen picture, with its formal linear treatment, its very restricted use of very deep shadows and extreme high lights, has given rise to a tendency in modern Western art which is not as fully appreciated by the layman as it is by some artists who object to the naturalistic picture which aims at a complete illusion by a futile attempt to imitate realities. The element of aërial perspective, which involves the change in the appearance of objects through loss of color as they are removed farther from the eye, is a highly overemphasized element in such pictures.

The decorative easel picture, on the other hand, is built up on entirely different principles. First of all it has little contrast in values, which in the eyes of many relegates it to the class of the poster. It derives its three-dimensional sense from linear rather than from aërial perspective. This in the main is the difference between a typical Chinese painting and a European painting of an imitative trend. It is often pointed out that, owing to the apparent simplicity, decorative paintings are an easy task. Everybody, we often hear, can make a decorative poster. Students in the schools make posters for many occasions. Sometimes they are truly beautiful, but often they are merely an affectation of a poorly digested principle. While the Oriental decorative picture renounces the use of

extreme gradations of shading and of light, most assuredly
it is not like the Western poster, in that it has the power of

MULBERRY AND COCOON

The frankly decorative treatment in this painting by Hoko Murakami is typical
of Oriental art. One distinctly feels here that every form has been carefully
studied with the idea of discovering beautiful patterns

suggesting depth by the intelligent use of linear perspective
developed in terms of design. To the untrained the greatest
compliment he can pay a picture is that the things in it actu-

ally seem to "stand out," as if the hand could feel all around them. Many artists, on the other hand, are most insistent in emphasizing a treatment by which the component parts of a picture appear to stand *in* but are not lacking in plastic feeling.

From Greek vase paintings, early Christian mosaics, the early Italians, down to Puvis de Chavannes and Whistler, the decorative principle has persisted, to be lost sight of every so often and to be reëmphasized in turn. The principle involved undoubtedly will be the bone of contention of future generations of artists and laymen. It is a very common attitude among laymen to ignore works of decorative character. The plastic modulation practiced by the popular painters of the Italian High Renaissance, who cultivated plastic representation with such baffling perfection, is a main cause of this neglect. It is only when the method of the so-called primitives is also taken into account that the shortcomings of these later Renaissance painters can be recognized. The beginner sees nothing but gain and pleasure in the work of Raphael or Leonardo or Titian, when he should also be conscious that the apparent struggling efforts of the earlier Byzantine painters more clearly adhere to some of the great principles of decoration, which ultimately became lost in the intoxication of technical skill and sophistication of the decadent painters of the Renaissance, such as Carlo Dolci, Correggio, and others.

In a survey of the history of painting it will be observed that the attitude of the artist toward the purpose of his work has many times shifted between the days of the early Italian and the present day. Giotto, among Renaissance painters, was the first in whose work emotional emphasis and expression of the subject predominated. While the later painter who painted Madonnas emphasized the religious fervor and exaltation of the subject represented, he most assuredly was not unconscious of the decorative elements. At present the formal treatment of subject matter has become the means by which the artist expresses his own concepts of beauty.

The modern stage setting, compared to the traditional setting of the past century, illustrates in another field the conflict between naturalistic imitation and the decorative. It is not so long ago that we expected in stage settings a most accurate physically descriptive imitation of nature. Our stage managers had to give the impression that the actors were walking under *real* trees; their dialogues were delivered from the tops of apparently real rocks, or from real tree stumps. All the stage properties had to be absolutely descriptive imitations of the real objects, produced with minute fidelity to all the accidental qualities in nature. It was the age of papier-mâché properties.

In recent years many distinguished stage managers all over the world have thrown these imitative properties into the discard; and our modern stage has become abstractly beautiful through true decoration, so conceived as to accentuate the mood (*Stimmung*) of the various parts of the play. The actor of today expresses the conflicts of the drama in a setting which is æsthetically a support to his words and actions,—not a distraction.

The conflict between the adherents of the merely imitative and of the decorative, in such of the arts as sculpture and painting and even the stage, is largely a cause of confusion in art appreciation, and this conflict also has contributed the basic factor in many revolutions in style which seem to occur at regular intervals. Unquestionably today the tendency in the representative arts is toward recognition of decoration as a desirable element. During the past, whenever the value of the decorative has been lost sight of, technical sophistication developed mannerisms which eventually became so extreme as to be unbearable and caused a reaction in the direction of the simple and the decorative. Every time the artistic profession becomes surfeited with mannerisms and excessive meaningless skill, when one art begins to trespass upon others, —when painting, for instance, encroaches upon literature,— this reaction toward the decorative seems inevitable.

MONA LISA

By Leonardo da Vinci. (Louvre, Paris)

Among art teachers the believers in imitation are yielding to the arguments for decoration as expressed in terms of design. However, training in many art schools still begins with imitation. The antique room, still-life painting, the portrait and life class, are the approach to the professional activities of the painter. The study of design—that is to say, the synthetic

A MODERN STAGE SETTING

A scene from "Helena's Husband," as staged at the Arts and Crafts Theater, Detroit, Michigan. The fine qualities of this design reflect the best standards of the modern stage

creating of beautiful forms as such—many modern teachers feel should be the first step in the training of every artist. The failure of many architects, sculptors, and painters is very often attributable to their inability to give beautiful and significant form to their work. What we call taste is essentially and intimately connected with the understanding of the principles of decoration, adornment. No artist in the past ever succeeded fully without the mastery of design, nor will any artist

A GLASS OF WINE

This modern American oil painting, by Raymond P. R. Neilson, suggests the
influence of Oriental art. Its charm is largely due to its pattern

in the future. The relegation of decorative design to the
craftsman, on the one hand, and the monopolizing of so-called
beautiful ideas to the exclusion of design, on the other, by the
academic painter are illogical. All art, whether it presents a

recognizable happening based upon life or not, must express itself in beautiful form; and formal beauty is bound up with decoration.

Naturalistic imitation in art, after having enjoyed a period of popular approval, always seems to be followed by a reaction in favor of decoration. The cycle has been completed several times already in art history. While Whistler marked the first suggestion of reaction in our own times, many moderns have surpassed him in the decorative use of form and color. If the decorative tendency of present-day art drifts again toward unselective naturalism, there will very likely be another cycle of reactions within a given time. On the other hand, the complaint today is often made, and perhaps not unjustly, that the fanatical demand for form alone, as expressed in pure decoration devoid of any characterization of the subject, is carried too far. The blame is laid at the door of the æsthetic theorist who insists upon making of art form a fetish and end in itself. The important thing for the student to remember is that the highest technical and character values are to be achieved only in a mutual relationship of both of these factors in artistic expression.

X

ORDER, COMPOSITION, DESIGN

In the social structure of which he is a part the person of but little acquaintance with art is not unmindful of the necessity of order: we all realize that society would disintegrate unless some system of order provided a place for each unit and governed its relation to others. Order, then, is concerned with the relationship of one unit to other units. At all times the need for order has been manifest to everyone who is concerned with the preservation of civilization. Before we turn to an analysis of order as a significant element in art, it will be desirable to arrive at this understanding regarding the importance of social order. Order is such relationship of component parts as to permit of the fullest development of the identity, the significance, the character, of each unit without injury to the others.

Nearly everyone has at times watched opposing parties in a football scrimmage eager to gain possession of the ball. The identity of each player to most observers under these circumstances becomes lost. The scene is one of great confusion, of marked disorder. On the other hand, a large number of individuals uniformed and drawn up in line present in a marked way the idea of order; the identity of the individual here is preserved perhaps to an uninteresting degree. In general, every normal individual feels that his life is unenjoyable and unprofitable under a condition of disorder. History, particularly recent history, offers many evidences that order as the law of heaven is indeed not practiced everywhere on earth. Confusion, disorder, is wasteful and, more than that, conducive to crime. Whenever society arrives at a state where the individual is difficult to identify, responsibility difficult to place, crime is likely to flourish.

Inversely, then, if we agree upon order as a fundamental requirement in life, the values to be derived from the study of art, in that it presents the law of order in its most appealing expressions, may well be recognized as applying to social relationships. The definitions of these laws of design, presented and exemplified in the following chapters dealing with the formal qualities of works of art, should then be comprehended in the larger sense in which order has been here discussed.

The habit of orderly thought is characteristic of the logician; the orderly arrangement of facts toward an æsthetic end is the formal aim of every artist.

Order as an art principle may perhaps be best defined, then, by stating that it is an arrangement of factors in accordance with some recognizable method. No matter what the particular method may be, so long as any be recognizable, order is recognizable. The process to the artist involves continuous experimentation,—observing, comparing, judging, arranging and rearranging.

In the diagram above we observe a variety of unrelated forms in an open field. They convey a marked sense of disorder. The effect would be one of even greater disorder if these forms appeared to cross one another.

The only noticeable improvement in the direction of order in the first diagram on page 119 is the result of using a definite field within which appear some of the forms used in the diagram on page 118. The forms are held together by a common boundary without artistic effect.

In the right-hand diagram below, some of the same forms appear with more recognizable relationship to the sides of the

inclosure. However, their relation to each other is still unsatisfactory and disorderly; in fact, if we are to establish an artistic relationship, we must change their form in the direction of harmony; that is to say, we must eliminate all conflicting shapes and concentrate upon one type without losing variety.

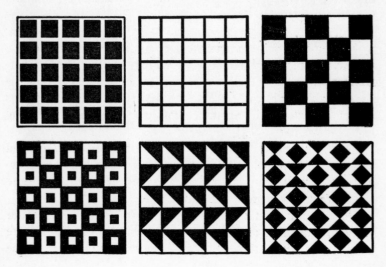

In the set of diagrams on page 119 order has been graphically expressed in the simplest terms possible. In the first diagram we have absolute order, but no contrast. The same is true of the second. In the third we recognize the well-known checkerboard, undoubtedly one of the oldest art expressions of absolute order, absolute contrast, and absolute harmony. The fourth, fifth, and sixth diagrams are modifications to illustrate what may be accomplished in very simple terms.

In this diagram we are now able to recognize order in its larger æsthetic significance, expressed in abstract forms but recognizable in principle, as in all representative art. The parts appear in a consistent relationship to each other and also to the inclosing frame. As compared to the first diagram this arrangement unquestionably is enjoyable. Incidentally, we have here harmony and symmetry, a discussion of which we must postpone to the following chapters. Order as expressed here, in terms of pure design, is in this instance an end in itself; while in the representative arts, such as sculpture or painting, it is but a means toward an end, the representation of some recognizable object being the other aim of these arts.

Nature, the godmother of the arts, presents to the artist many beautiful expressions of order in a great variety of organic forms, and every work of art resembles in some measure the system of structural organic order recognizable in a plant or animal. In nature an organic form, as compared to an inorganic form, is indicated in the traceable system in which are active the forces which influence every part of the organic form: plants and animals, with their complete circulatory systems, are organic; sand and stone are not. In many art forms

FLOWERS, PLANTS AND FISHES, BIRDS, BEASTS, FLYES &
BEES, THERES NOTHING NEERE AT HAND OR FARTHEST
SOUGHT BUT MAY BE WITH THE NEEDLE SHAP'D & WRAUGHT.

EMBROIDERED SCREEN

In this design by Ruth Rayner of London, England, the idea of organic development may readily be recognized

may be traced, if only faintly, either a vertical development,— very common in nature and art,—exemplifying order as graphically represented in the growing plant, or a horizontal development, as seen in the quadruped. We have come to expect of any work of art elements which represent its head, its body, and its ending. The study of art will disclose the fact that the master workers of all ages must have devoted a large part of their lives to the study of the organic construction of natural forms, and with the valuable knowledge thus gained they have been better able to demonstrate with courage and conviction their artistic ideas.

Now that we have been made conscious of order in the abstract as well as in nature, recognition of order in definite manifestations permits us to make a more systematic analysis of all the structural organic ideas in art; and since the term "composition" includes all these processes as indicated in the heading of this chapter, we will devote our attention here to an analysis of the several terms.

Composition is involved in all the arts: we speak of the creative musician as the composer, and the term "composition" is very commonly employed in literature. In fact, many of the obstacles in the path of art appreciation would be more readily overcome if we would learn to think of all artists as composers in some medium.

"Composition" is derived from the Latin word *componere*, meaning "to put together"; and every convincing work of art we find undergoes manifold constructive operations in the development from fragmentary sketches—ideas expressed in experimental form, as it were—to the definite and final product. The putting together of the various elements which make up a work of art offers, therefore, boundless opportunity for individual expression. To every artist, naturally, it is a most engrossing process. How formally to express himself in his chosen medium in such a manner as to give the greatest amount of æsthetic pleasure, and at the same time to preserve, through composition, by its manner of presentation, the spiritual, the inner, meaning of the subject—here is a task which offers the opportunity by which artists hope to attain a personal note and achieve distinction in their work.

CANDLESTICKS, MIRROR, AND FLOWER BOWL

A simple composition of beautiful objects. The student should endeavor to
realize the pleasing proportions and form of the candlesticks. The contrast of
horizontal and vertical lines is very striking

"Composition," then, as the word is used in the graphic
arts, has a meaning more far-reaching than any other term
emanating from the studio. It is to be expected that some will

interpose the thought that if the artist would be content to reproduce a thing as he saw it before him, he would not enlarge upon his many difficulties. In taking liberties with the natural material he often is suspected to be lacking in reverence for nature. It is indeed commendable to have such implicit faith in nature; but when one learns to appreciate some of the problems of the artist, one finds that not all the compositions of nature are adapted to use in art. The organic idea as exemplified by nature, to which we committed ourselves, must not be confounded with meaningless superficialities. The ability intelligently to apply the right principles in art requires an appreciation of the greatest wonders nature affords in a million ways to the searching student. Furthermore, nature as she exists is a great unity made up of things interrelated. Now let us imagine just a haphazard fragment of any great vista, as presented by mechanical photographic means, confined in a frame of rectangular proportions. It is manifestly a fragment. It has a meaning, but usually no composition; for nature has no frame. She is indefinite,—continuous, as it were. Her effects melt into one another in kaleidoscopic fashion. A subject seen out of doors appears altogether different from that the artist presents within the physical boundaries of a frame. This boundary, as expressed in geometrical forms which provide fixed definite limits for the picture, is the raison d'être for many laws of composition in the field of pure design as well as in representative painting.

The processes of photography are very helpful indeed in making clear some fundamental ideas about composition. The main difference between a fact recorded by ordinary mechanical photographic means and a fact interpreted by the artist on canvas lies in the noncommittal, equal emphasis of facts appearing in the photograph, as contrasted with the process of intelligent elimination, emphasis, subordination, or rearrangement of materials which has gone into the creation of the artist's work. The photographer, obviously, has not the freedom of arrangement that is within the means of the painter.

This is the reason why the photograph of the ordinary commercial type gives us so little æsthetic thrill. We acknowledge the information it presents, and perhaps, for practical purposes, we refer to it again, to refresh our minds; but it seldom makes any artistic appeal. We rarely think of it again.

MIRANDA ON THE BALCONY

This photograph, by Helen MacGregor, London, reveals to an unusual degree the artistic possibilities of photography through the exercise of a marked sense of design. A work of art has been created by means of a limited technique

The photograph which is reproduced here is typical of many thoughtfully taken by those workers who are conscious of the definite relation the material in a photograph assumes to the frame. The artistic photograph, in a large measure, then, is the result of the selective process employed by the artist.

It has experienced all the modification and arbitrary treatment a painter would give to his work, and it is therefore properly a work of art. It is a monochrome painting done in a fashion technically rather limited. Since the camera today is in such common use, it is instructive to illustrate the need of careful composition. The photograph affords a means of explanation better than reproductions of pictures, which are mostly without defects of composition and therefore of negative value only. Most paintings worthy of reproduction are an arbitrary but careful arrangement of facts, so selected as to emphasize the potential æsthetic elements furnished by nature and, at the same time, to stress one central phase of an idea.

The effect that different geometric boundaries have upon the mind is a very important factor in art. The square, of all forms, is perhaps the least interesting. As the two-dimensional version of the cube, it suggests the immobility of the parent form. While it suggests strength and resistance, it has little appeal to the pictorial artist, by reason of the absence of any contrast of proportion. In abstract design, particularly in all-over pattern, the square is a favorite; and, as we have demonstrated in the checkerboard and its derivations, it may be used to great advantage.

The rectangle differs from the square in that it has an element of variety, the result of the different length of its pairs of sides. These often indicate the relations produced by the golden section, of which we will say more in the chapter on rhythm. While the square is noncommittal as to direction, the rectangle has a directive effect upon the mind according to the manner of its use. Owing to its very marked sense of support and repose, the rectangle in which the difference of dimension in the pair of sides is great, if resting on its long side, becomes the logical boundary for all subjects expressing repose. The chaise longue, the davenport, the long library table, all illustrate the obvious qualities of the rectangle resting on the long side.

If used standing on end, the rectangle at once emphasizes verticality, even uplift, and correspondingly is used in architecture, sculpture, and painting whenever that quality is desirable. In the field of architecture towers, skyscrapers, everywhere illustrate the vertical feeling of the rectangle on end.

THE SAGE-BRUSH TRAIL

While the picture itself is rectangular, the important forms within it are built up on a pyramidal plan. (From the oil painting by Oscar E. Berninghaus)

The triangle is markedly static in its feeling. The elements contained within it may appear crowded, even confined at times to an uncomfortable degree. The triangle resting on its base is the well-known symbol of absolute repose. The Pyramids have demonstrated this quality throughout the ages. Triangular picture frames are very rare indeed. The triangle poised on one angle becomes most unsatisfactory to the eye by reason of its lack of stability. In decorative design it may appear in any possible position as long as some support is given by adjacent elements. Many-sided geometrical forms, like the hexagon, are frequently used and hold our interest, all such forms having a marked feeling of variety.

Of all forms the circle is one of the most beautiful, although it lacks variety. It possesses harmony to an absolute degree, all points of the circle being equidistant from the center. No more fascinating simple form exists than the sphere, and the circle carries with it all the qualities of movement and beauty belonging to the sphere; but, owing to its lack of a definite point of support, it sometimes gives the feeling of instability, particularly if the elements of form and color contained within it are used without judicious regard to balance. An unbalanced design within a circle only results in a sense of unceasing motion, suggesting the squirrel in the cage. Raphael, in the "Madonna della Sedia," and Michelangelo, in the "Holy Family," have shown us how to compose successfully within the circle. The ellipse, in pictorial boundaries as well as in decoration,—particularly in the shape of mirrors,—is a much-used form; it is in some respects more beautiful than the circle, but it also has obvious defects, particularly if used vertically. The ellipse is most enjoyable resting on the long axis. Combinations of the simple straight-line forms—such as the square, the rectangle, the triangle—with the circle are common, the variations thus gained possessing the qualities of their parent forms. The lunette æsthetically is most pleasing, possessing both the stability of the straight line and the beauty of the curvilinear form. All these forms are possible of endless combination, and the student will derive much pleasure from the study of all their applications in the applied arts.

It is evident that not only artists but also laymen must realize the æsthetic significance of the frame as such, and the student will always be rewarded by noting the harmonious proportions and profiles in the frames of James McNeill Whistler, and other artists who profited from his example. Very many frames fail to accentuate the qualities of the pictures contained within them: they have far too great a power of diverting the attention. A good frame does not dominate its painting. If the frame does not profitably accentuate the qualities of the picture, it should be content to act as a

MADONNA AND SAINTS
By Botticelli. (Uffizi, Florence)

neutralizing agent between it and the background against which it appears. Artists recognize the importance of the frame in two ways: as determining the physical boundaries of the picture and as a factor contributing character to a picture. The shapes of frames are obviously, then, governed by the compositional requirements of a subject.

Many a potential work of art has been spoiled by an attempt to adjust it to a wrongly proportioned frame. Certain motifs demand a vertical emphasis; others, a horizontal; others, again, some other emphasis. The vertical grandeur of a waterfall, or of a group of stately trees, is often enhanced in dignity by emphasizing, in the selection of the frame, the natural verticality of the subject. On the other hand, how stunted such arrangements appear if put into a square frame, which nullifies all vertical emphasis in the picture. Contrasted with this vertical development, we recall the horizontal composition, so common in marines or paintings of lowlands and marshes, where a certain horizontal indefiniteness and a feeling of repose are appropriate to the subject. In the case of some marines, we may have a rectangular composition of greater height than breadth, if an expansive sky above the water is more important than the ocean itself; or, if there is hardly any sky, but only a boldly patterned water surface, the marine, by reason of its detached interest, is well confined in an almost square canvas. In general, however, the marine lends itself best to a horizontal composition.

There exists, thus, a definite relation between the shape of the frame and the composition of the picture. Our compositional laws are all, within these shapes, guided by the system of construction and behavior of living forms, particularly of the human body and of plant structures, especially if the development be vertical. In fact, most of our æsthetic laws indicate a definite physiological origin. Every condition in a work of art suggesting physical discomfort is æsthetically unsatisfactory; while all suggestive of firm support lead to a sense of repose, the consistent relationship of parts develops harmony, and the accessibility of elements promotes rhythm. All these principles may thus be said to parallel those underlying organic life and growth.

The treatment pictorially of the part of a picture which borders upon the lower horizontal line is often secondary, and in form merely a starting-point physically. It serves the purpose of introduction, preparation; it is like the foundations of the house, or the pedestal supporting sculpture.

As we analyze any work of art, we meet with a gradual development of energies, a loosening of form, a certain attempt at gesticulation and expression. The lower part of the body furnishes the foundation, the support, for the activities and movements of expression which culminate in the upper part, often represented in the head. When a work of art is divided into halves by a vertical line, it will often reveal equal opposing forces, as in a human figure; if it is horizontally divided, it reveals no such relationship. We have compared the composition of a work of art of vertical growth to a plant or a tree, for it has the same upward growth from basal stability, as exemplified by the roots, to the increased activity and life of the upper parts, ultimately finding its most significant expression in the flower. In architecture, sculpture, and painting we often find, then, the expressive movement and forms of the composition above the immobile and stationary region of the foreground.

Our examination of a picture generally begins with the base, because of association of ideas derived from nature. We analyze the picture or the statue or the building from below,—seldom from either side or from the top. The general scheme of distribution of force in many compositions may be recognized as a horizontal base supporting a vertical element. This principle applies in the main to compositions of architecture, sculpture, and paintings of greater height than width, and to those which are square. Compositions of greater width than height will offer very little opportunity for a vertical development. As has been indicated by our discussion of geometric boundaries, the shape of pictures is of the utmost æsthetic significance. The artist not infrequently keeps in reserve canvases of many proportions and many sizes, from which he selects with great discrimination. He realizes that the relation of the subject matter in a picture to the four sides of the canvas is the first and most important consideration. How important this is, and how difficult it is to gauge absolutely the final effect of a composition, may be demonstrated by the fact that some of our most experienced artists occasionally feel the necessity for altering the shape of their pictures after having proceeded beyond the preliminary stage. How many pictures

BY THE RIVER

This painting, by Joseph T. Pearson, Jr., is strictly conceived in terms of decoration

have been cut down in size or altered in their proportions, in order to adjust their composition, we do not know unless we examine the edges of the picture hidden under the frame. But many canvases of the old masters have had pieces of canvas added to them after they were carried far toward completion. While every artist is conscious of the relations discussed above, mistakes are sometimes made by the stretching of a scant motif over a disproportionately large surface. The intrinsic interest in the motif, then, must be properly related to the area in which a work of art appears. Many large pictures look very much more interesting if reduced to a small scale by photographic means; on the other hand, the enlargement of a picture through the stereopticon lantern may so dilute its attractive qualities that its effect becomes impaired. These diluted art expressions result from a lack of judgment on the part of the artist; and whether met with in music, sculpture, or painting, the effect is precisely as in the case of the unduly enlarged stereopticon view, or in those books which contain only enough elements of interest for a short article.

While Benjamin West impressed his contemporaries with his colossal paintings, it is generally felt today that he failed to impart interest to his needlessly large canvases. The size of a picture in pictorial art, then, assumes the importance of a special problem. Obviously it would be much less troublesome to the artist to have certain definite sizes, agreed upon among art workers; but the requirements of different subjects vary so much that any such uniformity is manifestly impossible.

It is a most fascinating pleasure, afforded too seldom to the student, to watch the compositional growth of a picture, from the sketchy foundation to its completion; for few compositions remain the same through their many evolutionary stages. To find a pictorially effective composition in nature and transfer it to a canvas is rarely possible, although we do meet occasionally with what we speak of as paintable subjects, as opposed to those which are not paintable,—those which are often called picturesque scenes by the layman. When the artist uses the term "picturesque," he does not necessarily mean an interesting occurrence, but often merely compositional opportunities. Certain sections of the world, such as Holland, have for many years been sketching-grounds for painters on account of the simple arrangement of their out-of-doors. On the other hand, the complex contortions of a tropical landscape will offer charms only to persons insensible to order as a necessity to art form. Simplicity is a desirable feature which the artist knows he cannot neglect, even in the spectacular. For the same reason, a good composition requires a simple and interesting contrast of light and dark, and a good silhouette is effective in expressing the character of a person.

It is claimed for the art of the present day that it pays a good deal more attention to composition than that of many previous periods,—a fact which may be explained by the growing importance of the decorative picture. Although modern art does not manifest itself in the grandiose compositions we recognize in the work of Michelangelo or Raphael, its emphasis of design is quite evident. The pure joys of abstract beauty of line and form and color seem to appeal to the artist now more than ever; though they continue to offer the most difficult problem to the layman, on account of his lack of training in such matters rather than his lack of inherent artistic perception. It is the purely abstract quality of the appeal in Japanese art which has always stood between it and the Western public.

The primary importance of the subject of composition further becomes manifest when one considers that no attention can be paid by any artist to mere detail until the location of each form within the composition is definitely established. The partly finished works of many artists, in all media, have shown us the variety of experimental changes which pictures suffer in their development toward the final form. Oftentimes a sketch or study will possess a charm, suggested by experiment, which the finished picture, devoid of many accidental qualities and turned cold and inanimate, lacks.

XI

SYMMETRY; BALANCE

Order, expressed in balance, enters into all the arts. While we may have balance of interest to a certain degree in the arts that move in time, such as music, poetry, and the drama, the problem assumes particular importance in the space arts—architecture and sculpture, because in these arts the different elements possess a varying amount of physical weight.

However, in every work of art the content and form elements each have a definite power of attraction, and when these elements are opposed in such a way as to result in a condition of equilibrium, we feel a composition as properly balanced. They may be disposed of in an infinite number of ways that engage our attention in a consideration of balance.

Absolute balance—that is to say, absolute symmetry—is usually employed only in monumental architecture, in order to achieve an effect of central emphasis of simple dignity. Such absolute balance seems appropriate to the function of many architectural units as a central axial pivoting-point. A great number of monumental buildings, like the Lincoln Memorial or the Capitol in Washington, are designed on this principle. If we draw an imaginary vertical line through the center of such structures, the two resulting halves will be found to be exactly alike.

In thinking of balance of this kind we visualize at once the ordinary scales for weighing materials, and these will assist in illustrating the most common method of balance in art. That is to say, an ordinary scale, consisting of two arms of equal length, supporting equal amounts of the same substance, will find its counterpart in many works of architecture and other compositions, resulting in absolute symmetry upon a vertical basis. However, it is well known that such a scale may also maintain perfect equilibrium if one arm carries a pound of lead and the other a pound of feathers. The pound weight, after all, is a pound; and as long as the mind is conscious of the idea of equal weight, the physical size of the substances weighed may vary and still a sense of equilibrium may prevail.

The opposition of objects dissimilar in appearance but of equal force of attraction appears to be the aim of the pictorial artist striving for originality and variety. In the practical solution of the problem of pictorial balance, there are possible a great many interesting modifications and variations. Line, form, color, light and dark, may all be set in play against each other, in order to distribute the interest equally within the frame. The powers of sentimental appeal must here also be recognized as playing an important part in the matter of balance; the importance of every object, in so far as it exerts a pull upon our attention, must be carefully weighed. The social rank, physiognomy, size, and action of a person may all call for proper adjustment of a pictorial composition, in order to insure balance. Distribution of similar objects in even or uneven numbers often seriously engages painters before they ever think of their detailed expression.

Although the simplest, most obvious way of creating balance in any art, as has already been pointed out, is to make both halves absolutely alike, it will readily be seen that balance of that kind, while desirable in architecture, is likely to be uninteresting in a picture, with its definite, inflexible frame. Recognizing the desirability of variety, the painter's ingenuity, in order to meet this requirement, is confronted with a task which calls into action all his resources. To begin with the simplest graphic expression, the line: the artist through observation knows that shapes bounded by perfectly quiet lines will very easily be outweighed in interest by those characterized by curved or animated lines; for straight lines, in their lack of interest, do not excite us as do curved or animated lines. One may study this phenomenon best in some form of pure

MADONNA DEL BALDACCHINO

A convincing demonstration of the obvious means of securing symmetry and balance. (Painted by Raphael)

design, like an Oriental rug. The difference of character in the two types of line we shall have to deal with again while investigating the element of rhythm. It is sufficient here to state that the difference is so marked that an excessive employment of curved lines in one part of a composition may easily lead to conditions of unbalance. As in the case of all the laws of art, balance manifests itself in a subtle rather than a literal way; but close examination will train one to observe readily all its manifestations.

In pictorial compositions an effort is made to assemble pleasingly all the elements within the restricted space defined by the frame. Within this compass the eye establishes the physical pivoting-point upon which all the many factors are balanced. This point is in most cases near the center. If the two diagonals are drawn across a painting, the most engrossing points of interest will often be found grouped very near this focal point.

The most artistic effect of balance, then, is the result of the placing of apparently different things of similar attention value at about the same relative distance on either side of the central features of a picture.

We not infrequently find the Madonna, the king, the president, and other dignitaries assigned to the middle of the composition, because in the ensemble they are usually the most commanding figures. Single out the socially most prominent person in a figure composition, and rarely, in any well-balanced picture, is it far away from the center of the canvas. If it is not found in the place of greatest importance, its own importance obviously is impaired, unless it is the artist's intention to have one more equally important group on the other side of the center. The arrangement of actors on the dramatic stage offers a constantly changing opportunity for investigations of this sort. This point will not seem important until the violation of this rule of balance has once offended the sensibilities of the student.

The "Sistine Madonna," like so many Madonna pictures, reveals perfect balance—balance, to be sure, of the almost symmetrical kind—in the divided curtain. The Christ Child is opposed by the arm and the headdress falling to the left

CORONATION OF THE VIRGIN

By Velásquez. (Prado, Madrid)

shoulder. The figures of Pope Sixtus on the left and of Santa Barbara on the right attract equally, while the cherubs at the base are so nearly balanced in interest that they appear symmetrical. This picture is so clearly an example of the simple and effective type of balance that we must always admire it for its daring simplicity. Many Renaissance artists availed themselves of the compositional methods of Raphael, without achieving the simple style of his best work. Our drawings of symmetrical arrangements, on the preceding and following pages, present the more common schemes recognizable in pictorial composition. Symmetry in all these is recognizable in its consistent relation to a vertical dividing-line. Other reproductions of works of art used in this book will be found to be based upon these schemes. The commonest and most satisfactory of all symmetrical arrangements within a frame will be recognized in the triangle. To understand its very wide use, one must become conscious of the stability it gives to compositions. The pyramid has that quality of support which gives stability and poise to a work of art, and its extraordinarily frequent use should not cause surprise. In architecture, since earliest time, the pyramid has withstood every agency of destruction; it has become the symbol of static repose.

Practically every picture submits in its compositional arrangements to some definite scheme, and other forms than the triangle—particularly the circle, the cross, or the letter S— are recognizable in many pictorial schemes. These forms themselves are capable of modifications. The triangle may appear as very pointed or very obtuse; the circle may assume the shape of an oval, as if seen in perspective. The letter S may be recognized as a very elegant curve or a flat zigzag. These forms may be indicated either alone or in combination with one another. The aim always is to achieve some recognizable scheme of arrangement. This aspect of composition is best appreciated through the study of large numbers of pictures. The well-trained artist invariably achieves compositional balance, so that examples of failure in this respect are relatively rare.

When color is added to forms or areas, the problem becomes more complicated and more difficult, the general rule being that a form of animated outline, associated with light and color, will attract more attention and have more weight than a form of quieter outline and dark tone. The analysis of any monochrome reproduction of a painting will disclose this fact very quickly. Light faces, hands, the extremities generally, will much more quickly draw attention than the larger, quieter masses. For that reason we find lighter elements in pictures often assembled near the center. The lighter and more animated any part of a picture is, the more likely are we to find it there, particularly if there is only one such element in the picture. Exceptions to the rule occur in cases where several areas of light appear in different parts of a picture; in this instance we may observe some opposing arrangement upon a central axis.

In regard to the distribution of the quantities of light and dark, and the balance maintained between them, it will be observed that the darker masses of a picture generally exceed the lighter in quantity, since a very much larger amount of dark is necessary to balance a lighter and more animated spot in a picture. It is a bit of common knowledge, in the matter of dress, that white is inadvisable to anyone inclined toward stoutness and that a dark dress is likely to be unbecoming to the thin person, since the white tends toward larger and the dark color toward smaller appearance. In fact, light seems to eat into its surroundings. What is true on the street is true in the picture; the effect there is precisely the same. In a crowd on the street, half a dozen people in dark conventional garb will not offer as much interest as one person brightly and gayly clad. This question of light and dark is intimately connected with color, naturally; and where dark tones are associated with dull colors one's attention will not be stirred, while the combination of light tones and brilliant colors will most pronouncedly attract us. The elements in a picture are assembled with due regard for these principles.

A Corot landscape will seldom have the figure with the red bonnet far from the middle. An Inness landscape usually has its strongest emphasis in the middle. Many poetic moonlights present the illuminated window near the center, and every brilliant, lively note is usually found not far from it. This is true in the dark pictures of the older schools, but is no less so in those of the moderns, which, in spite of their "all over" quality of animation, have a central emphasis. The picture demands this centralization of interest if it is to maintain its equilibrium. It is for this reason that the painter speaks of a "pattern" in a picture; he means by this a synthetically constructed arrangement. Only the beginner will put the brightest-colored cow in the herd near the outside of the group, and all his protestations to his teacher that the cow was actually there will not help him with his intelligent critic, who knows that unless there is another equally attractive element on the other side of the center, making a similar spot, there will be no balance. In the still-lifes by Carlsen, Chase, or Breckenridge the emphatic color, the lively movement of form, is found near the center. In figure pictures, particularly in the case of drapery, much interest can be given by the opposition of stuffs of differing hue, such as red and blue, but of the same value and intensity. It is quite conceivable that a blue is outweighed on the opposite side by a similar quantity of red of the same strength or interest, and this example must be sufficient to suggest the endless possibilities in this direction.

On the other hand, another kind of scale, the steelyard, in which the supporting point is removed from the center and the two arms are of different lengths, represents a more unusual but not less interesting system of balancing the various elements of attraction in a painting. According to the principles governing this type of scale, it is dependent upon the opposition of a greater weight on the short arm and a lesser on the longer arm. The accompanying picture by Dixon, and also the well-known painting of Madame Récamier, by David, in the Louvre, illustrate this type. The point of support as established by the eye is not in the center of these pictures but in a vertical line to the left of the center. Compared with the first method this is comparatively uncommon, but in a discussion

of balance it cannot be ignored. However, there is still a
third method, in which slanting lines of interest are set to play
against each other, in order to achieve a sense of equilibrium.
These lines are likely to run diagonally across the composition, and they are identified and traceable through the points

WHAT AN INDIAN THINKS

An example of obtaining balance on the steelyard principle. The quiet dignity
of the figure is in harmony with the hour of the day. (From the oil painting by
Maynard Dixon)

of interest in it. The idea may be recognized in the picture by
Rubens, on page 144, over which these suggested lines have
been drawn in white. The picture by Higgins, on page 146,
also illustrates this principle. We note that a strongly marked
line running from the lower left to the upper right is balanced
by a number of minor lines running in the opposite direction.
This principle accounts for many subtle arrangements.

The preliminary sketch for any ambitious composition, whether architectural, pictorial, or sculptural, is also the most important step, because it is here that the balancing of masses

THE DAUGHTERS OF LEUCIPPUS

Balance through opposition of slanting lines. Painting by Rubens. (Old Pinakothek, Munich)

of light and dark must be determined, without any attention to the detailed delineation of the individual elements involved.

The larger the painting the more urgent becomes the necessity for the consideration of balance. In mural paintings particularly, architectural conditions also have to be considered,

THE ASSUMPTION OF THE VIRGIN

A scholarly composition in a well-designed frame which adds much to the effect of the picture. By El Greco. (The Art Institute of Chicago)

and the balancing of all elements becomes an absolute necessity. In "The Last Supper," by Leonardo da Vinci, the architectural background is practically the same on the two sides. The figure of Christ is exactly in the center, seated behind an

JUAN DOMINGO AND THE BREAD JAR

A strikingly bold contrast of light and dark. A strongly marked line of interest running from the lower left to the upper right corner is opposed by several minor lines running in opposite directions, as suggested in the position of the arms. (From the oil painting by Victor Higgins)

absolutely symmetrical table; the twelve disciples are equally divided in number on each side of the Master. In fact, the distribution of the elements of attraction is so very obvious that even an untrained person will be able to analyze this stately composition without any difficulty. But how has the artist succeeded in giving variety to this apparently mechanical distribution of pictorial elements? Largely by the skillfully used, highly characterized shapes of the figures of the disciples around the table. They are arranged in groups of threes, two such groups on each side. However, each group is so very different in itself that a feeling of sameness does not exist.

We find, then, that balance most commonly is maintained by the opposition of equal attractions, as represented by purely abstract elements (line, form, or color) and by content elements; second, by opposition of these elements on the steelyard principle; and, third, by their opposition on slanting opposing lines of interest. The possibilities of variation in balance, as in any artistic constituent, are endless, and to the student it is profitable to examine carefully many pictures from this point of view.

XII

RHYTHM IN ART AND IN NATURE

The element at once the most universal and most pleasurable in art discloses itself in the æsthetic manifestation we call rhythm. It furnishes one of the most stirring qualities in music and poetry, and it is through rhythm that we infuse musical qualities into the visually enjoyable arts. While balance is essentially a constructive necessity in a work of art, yielding the pleasure that comes with the contemplation of good order and the symmetrical opposition of elements, and while harmony causes agreeable emotional effects in its consistent use of forms and colors, neither one in its appeal is to be compared to the intense delight which springs from the rhythmic charm we may discern, in a greater or less degree, in architecture, sculpture, or painting, and in many minor arts. While balance and harmony must be present in a work of art if it is to be enjoyable in its structural meaning, rhythm is an almost indispensable quality in the artistic formulation of an idea.

The term "rhythm" in the visually enjoyable arts may be said to include several distinct manifestations. In the original —the larger and most important—sense it signifies a measured flow, a regularly repeated movement or beat, leading the eye or ear insistently from one part of a pictorial or musical composition to certain others. Second, it has come to mean any feeling of movement caused by association of ideas; any device, not strictly rhythmic in the sense of music or poetry, but causing the feeling of movement, is regarded by the painter as rhythmical. In a minor sense it has come to imply a certain clarity of arrangement of the subject matter expressing an instinct for order, which we usually recognize in any æs-

thetic law. Order, as we have seen, demands that we be able to find our way through the many parts of a composition fluently, uninterruptedly, and without interference.

Rhythm in the last sense has already been explained, in a chapter dealing with composition. We know that a composition must be planned so as to result in an orderly arrangement which will permit an enjoyment of the various parts in a systematic way, free from confusion. Owing to the placing of emphasis upon certain elements in all art expressions and to the subordination of other parts, rhythm is often employed to direct the attention to the important elements and, inversely, away from the unimportant.

In order to clarify rhythm in its larger meaning in the mind of the student, the drawings on page 149 may serve as an illustration. Rhythm here has been set forth in the simplest abstract form. It will be noted that a straight line is not suggestive of movement. The straight line, to our minds, however, has a course of direction from left to right, owing to the fact that we usually see it made that way. By giving it the well-known characteristics of an arrow it markedly gains in a sense of direction. A deviation from the straight, particularly the regularly undulating line, gives a sense of movement. We remember here the fundamental difference between the parent forms, the square and the circle. In design the use of the horizontal undulating line, as well as the vertical, is extremely common. These recurring lines must not, however, be too violent, as any violent curve—like the hairpin turn, known to the automobilist—is dangerous to the safe continuance of movement.

The increase or decrease in similar, related, or harmonious forms is another frequent method in causing a sense of movement in the visual arts. This movement may be accentuated by giving the element toward which the movement is directed an increased importance. In fact, any recognizable measured increase or decrease in attention conveys the impression of movement. In architecture this is illustrated in the measured gradual decrease of height of stories in a tower, or, in furniture, in the gradual decrease upward in the height of the drawers of a bureau. Rhythm is produced by units, each one having by itself the power to lead the eye toward a given point; so that if used in regular intervals, equal or progressively increasing or decreasing, they may acquire a considerable force of motion.

The element of rhythm in its larger meaning of pleasurable, consistent movement will become clearer if we make an excursion into nature for further examples. The most widely recognized factor in creating rhythm in nature is perspective, both linear and aërial. We all know that things seem to

TABLE AND BOWL

The consistent use of curvilinear forms is very agreeable

become gradually smaller as they recede; objects of the same kind, size, and dimension, like a row of trees of equal size, seem to diminish gradually with a most charming regularity and consistency. The wooden posts paralleling the row of trees follow the same law, as does the road, which seems to narrow down systematically toward a common point of confluence on the horizon opposite the spectator. To complete the picture, the equidistant telegraph poles on the opposite side, the car tracks in the middle of the road, all tend to take possession of one's interest, and all with the sole aim of forcing one's attention to a certain point in the distance. The nature of rhythm clearly is established if one surrenders oneself to the overpowering control of converging lines. In the many religious pictures of the Renaissance this confluence of lines, caused by objects represented in perspective, is a very common means of leading the beholder's eye from the foreground toward the point reserved for the Madonna and the Christ Child. In the monumental architectural wall and ceiling decorations of the Renaissance, and wherever linear perspective is much in evidence, it has always been used as a most effective device.

It is unquestionably much more interesting to see great numbers of the same things, like voids and solids in a façade, in gradually decreasing sizes than to have them all appear of the same size. This effect of rhythm in stimulating interest is well illustrated by comparing the effect upon us of the architectural drawing of the so-called "front elevation" type, stiff and monotonous in its regularity, with that of the perspective drawing, with its rhythmically disappearing apertures. The architect appreciates that the former makes little pleasurable impression; the latter is much insisted upon by his client, who seems to have a definite feeling for the rhythmic charm of converging lines and spaces.

Similarly in other art forms, the systematic increase or decrease of the size of objects, as they are affected by perspective, offers an unlimited expression of beauty which many people scarcely sense, though many similar phenomena in nature are properly considered most fascinating. The appeal of these natural phenomena, while they are seldom rhythmical in the accurate sense of the word, is often closely connected with rhythm in the sense that they possess the power pleasurably to attract our attention. The clouds in the sky, particularly the cirro-cumuli, are most engrossing in their subtle gradation of decreasing volume. Many pleasing skies in pictures seem less accidental in their design when one studies the carefully carried-out formula of gradually increasing or decreasing cloud formation. Again, the sea, with its unceasing motion, has more of true rhythmic movement than any other of nature's Protean expressions. The gradual collapse of the high waves, spending their last energies away up on the sand in faint ripples, has the irresistible fascination of movement

THE OPEN SEA
By Emil Carlsen. (The Minneapolis Institute of Art)

which, as soon as spent, is recreated by a never-ceasing force. There is something typically rhythmic in the manifold suggestion of movement disclosed in the activities of the waters surging around the shore. Movement runs through every part of the immediate shore land, not alone through the water itself. The charming decrease in volume which leads one from the far-out breakers gradually in to the lapping shore waves is very pleasurable, and the meaning of its charm of systematic change is recognizable in many other features. The sand on the beach, with its indentations remaining from the eddying tide, becomes much more interesting when once one recognizes the rhythm of its linear and form alignment. Farther up the beach, even débris is disposed in curving linear arrangements of unmistakable rhythmic charm. Pebble beaches are enchanting, with their multicolored stones, which seem to have been arranged with due regard for gradual increase or decrease in size. The smaller ones, those which are easily moved, are near the water; the bigger ones, higher up on the beach: it is as if they were all assorted and arranged by some skilled hand. This sense of rhythmical movement may be enjoyed also in many plant forms. The graceful charm of drooping trees, in the pendulous quality of the weeping willow, in the more agitated but nevertheless consistent feeling of movement in trees that have bent before the wind,—all this becomes more pleasurable once the quality of the rhythm is realized. The eucalyptus tree in its leaves demonstrates a principle of growth in rhythmic terms recognizable in nature in a hundred different ways. One may find many more such examples of expressions of rhythm in nature; but these will serve to show that the systematic gradual increase or decrease in the size of an object, whether produced by perspective or by actual physical difference of size, will set the attention in motion, traveling from the smaller toward the larger, or vice versa, according to the attracting value the forms possess.

Theoretically speaking the commonest method in art of creating a feeling of movement is in the alternation of a large unit in a design with a small one, and the repeating of this arrangement indefinitely. One travels from the large to the small with accelerated motion, to be caught, possibly, by some other modifications of this device which will lead one back. The undulating line, as we have seen, is the artistic line: it has life. The straight line is lifeless. It is this fact which for all time has settled the superior artistic value of Venus over Apollo: man is "square." There is no doubt that the practice of most painters of the academic schools, of drawing in curved lines to round out and fill corners, is due to the greater artistic significance of the curved line. The use of curved lines gives that element to a composition which we may call swing, that verve of motion which agitates us pleasantly and which gives a work of art dynamic force.

We may be stimulated by the simple device of increasing the interest of a picture in a certain direction by intensifying color. A more or less differentiated pattern, gradually lengthened in its design and intensified in its color, will draw the eye from the lightly developed part toward the more expressive. Many a purely decorative design in a rug will disclose this effect convincingly; any sunset will demonstrate this, also. The converging lines of the rays, assisted by the increase of intensity of color toward the point of convergence, culminating in the red, fiery ball, is so compelling that the sun seems almost like a bloody symbol of the crash of mighty forces which culminate in it. After you once get to the sun you can't get away from it. The eye gradually is released by the disappearance of the spectacle. The sunset not only illustrates again the dominant quality of converging lines, assisted by the increase in color intensity in the direction of their convergence, but also shows that it is very easy to lead the beholder of a pictorial composition to a point from which there is no escape. Since a picture is something different from a section cut out from nature, it must provide a means of allowing the eye to travel through all the parts associated within the frame. A cul-de-sac, such as we find in the sunset picture, is not desirable; there ought to be a chance for a return. Every part must be visually accessible, in a way to produce in the beholder the pleasures of contrast of light and dark, of important and unimportant, or of other opposed elements.

It is this element of movement inherent in the opportunities furnished by the management of line, space, and color which the true artist recognizes as his most valuable asset. It was neglected in the representations of the Düsseldorf school of genre painters, who were so absorbed in the facial expressions in their figural pictures that a pure abstract beauty in their work rarely could mature. How much more rhythmic are the pictures of the Pre-Raphaelites! What a wonderful play of swinging lines is there in Albert Moore's goddesses or in the ephemeral figures of Dante Gabriel Rossetti! In fact, many of the followers of the brotherhood had the instinctive feeling for the swinging, musical line.

The most interesting expressions of rhythm are found in the purely decorative figure studies of Whistler. Even those who have no conception of the meaning of rhythm could not help succumbing to the charm of his most tenuous sketches and studies. These slightly indicated figures may have no faces— merely heads, without features to express joy, grief, concern, fright; they need tell no story; their hands may be undivided masses, and the drawing of their feet similarly undeveloped. But what a compelling rhythmic charm radiates from them! Their poses make them reach for one another. They speak to one another without visible means of communication. The sources of their charm are all rhythmic movement, suggesting invisible forces tying together the simple, suggestive figures.

There are exceptions where an artist does not care to lead the eye over a certain road of attraction within a composition, and it may easily happen that interest is still carried through and outside the picture. In some of the landscapes of Millet, Corot, Inness, where storm is the theme, the movement is often of this kind. In most compositions, however, the line of movement is definitely aimed to lead the attention within the picture over a well-defined road. Any good picture will meet this test, though rhythm, in the sense of movement, may not be used obviously. For example, in "The Forge of Vulcan," by Velásquez, at Madrid, the eyes are carried in an elliptical path from head to head, passing over the anvil and back again. In figure painting it is particularly Rembrandt, as in his "Lesson in Anatomy," at The Hague, who shows how to manipulate many heads in a picture in a similar way so as to avoid confusion and to enable one to travel on a circular or elliptical path, from head to head and back to the starting-point, with remarkable ease. The chapter dealing with balance should here be remembered. Rembrandt's method was largely that of making his pictures simple and pushing everything back into the obscurity of his luminous background.

THE JOLLY ROGER

The measures of light and dark are very rhythmical. (Photograph by Helen MacGregor)

It must be clear, then, that rhythm in the larger meaning, that of sustained movement which carries the eye through sympathetic areas and along beautiful lines, is much more unusual in pictorial art than it is in pure design. But if it is attained through the use of rhythmic decorative pattern on costumes and dress generally, a picture may be very beautiful merely as a rhythmic design, irrespective of an intellectual meaning. John W. Alexander's "Pot of Basil," at Boston, or his "Phyllis," at St. Louis, are unusually typical of the qualities of movement enjoyed in pictorial compositions through the use of fluent lines. The folds of the gowns, while perfectly natural, are so effectively arranged as to give one pleasure also as spaces and as lines. Here the artist adds his knowledge to nature as only such a designer as Alexander could do it.

THE STORM

Earth and sky are patterned to express motion in this painting. (By Hermann Dudley Murphy)

Methods of producing rhythm in the sense of movement in a picture, then, are as numerous as they are subtle. Aside from the gradual intensification of color, there may be observed the gradual reduction or increase of tone in a picture, whereby the eye begins with either the darkest or the lightest points in a picture and gradually follows the scale of increasing or decreasing values, as the case may be. Commonly this increase or decrease of values leads toward the important point in the picture. With this increase or decrease in value, one must think of the assistance given to that suggested movement by perspective. Any normal eye will naturally, owing either to habit or to optical necessity, look first at those parts in a picture which are represented as being closest to the eye. This progress is accelerated by reduction in color : by giving those things in the foreground the most brilliant colors, and those farthest

SUMMER EVENING ON THE RIVER

This picture by Gustav Fjäestad is conspicuous for its emphasis of rhythmic forms. (Minneapolis Institute of Art)

away little or no color, the loss being very gradual. The decrease in the size of things, due to perspective, is so systematic as to be subject to a fixed law; the artist, having recognized this, makes use of it in many ways. The scientist has expressed this principle in the rule of the golden section, by which a whole is divided into two parts with the result that the smaller part is related to the bigger as the bigger to the sum total. This particular relation of parts, as expressed in the golden section, is a basic element in rhythm. To draw the attention to the focal point in a composition, a device often employed, then, is gradual increase or decrease in size and also in intensity of color. Some of the most trivial and ordinary of objects are often appealing to the artist because of their artistic quality of rhythm, suggested by that wonderfully interesting relation of areas which leads the eye pleasantly through any arrangement of forms endowed with artistic quality.

ALLEGRETTO

Etching by Cleo Damianakes

Artists like Hokusai, in his picture of "The Wave," with Fuji in the distance, have demonstrated the beauty of this law to perfection. All good marine painters know that and utilize it, as the works of Homer, Carlsen, Woodbury, Dougherty, Waugh, and Ritschel show. In a well-composed sky we are led from the bigger clouds above us to the smaller near the horizon,—particularly on a moonlight night, where there are cirrus clouds above, which seem gradually to dwindle away into the dark horizon. It is in the conscious application of rhythm to his expressions of natural phenomena that the painter may make his work appealing whenever he wants to; for nature's rhythm occurs only at times, while the artist can produce it whenever he will.

While we may usually think of rhythm as the main æsthetic force in poetry, music, and the dance, it must be recognized also as a very significant contributing factor in architecture, sculpture, and painting. All three of these first-named arts, so to speak, move in time, and therefore have an additional, and in one way physical, sense of movement behind them which makes rhythm even more impelling. The rhythm in the other arts, however, while less conspicuous, is no less important.

In modern days, rhythm is being emphasized in many activities in life on the ground that it actively promotes physical well-being. The cultivation of rhythm is being advocated as a cure for mental and physical ills. There are schools of rhythmic thinking and physical training, all aiming at the classic ideal of spiritual and physical perfection. Our "manners," in so far as they possess grace and charm, are undoubtedly the result of the recognition of rhythm as a desirable attribute. Although the much-caricatured practice of rhythmic formality as expressed in bows and curtsies seems an affectation to many of us, we cannot deny the charm of the rhythmic, fluent, elegant manner of some people as compared with that of others, whose formal actions are often less polished, even objectionable, unrhythmic.

The undeniable importance of rhythm in practical life suggests at once the many desirable qualities one may at every turn derive from a study of art. In the broadest sense, rhythm is the living quality in all things.

XIII

HARMONY—UNITY

In emphasizing, as we have in an earlier chapter, the necessity for structural order in a work of art, we have indicated that the elements in themselves which may express order are of a very great variety. Aside from a definite scheme of organic or structural relationship, these various formal factors must, if they are to appeal to us, be harmoniously related among themselves. Harmony as an expression of order is no less appreciated in human affairs than it is in art, and we once more recognize an æsthetic law based upon human experience and relationship. Harmony, as an expression of consistent and agreeable relationship among humans, is an absolute necessity. The individual radically out of harmony with society eventually will find himself in conflict with the laws, unless he retires to an uninhabited island where he is spared contact with other human beings. It will not be questioned that harmony is a necessary and desirable element, and we are made distinctly conscious of it in the contemplation of a work of art. Obviously, then, the first requirement we should insist upon in artistic objects devoted to practical use is that these objects should be in harmony with their purpose. However, as we have pointed out in discussing the grotesque, this necessity is not always recognized. Sentiment, either real or assumed, is oftentimes the cause of the preservation of many things out of harmony with their alleged uses, which, looked at apart from sentiment, are often shocking expressions of bad taste.

It has been said that harmony evolves from fitness, adaptability to other units, consistency with general purpose; and we shall see how in the more general field of pictorial art the law of harmony has become one of the most essential requirements for æsthetic enjoyment. Unfortunately, harmony in the mind of the layman is identified only with music and, perhaps, color. In music it signifies a concord of sounds, a combination of parts resulting in an effect æsthetically pleasing. And in all the arts *harmony*, in this latter sense of "a combination of parts resulting in an effect æsthetically pleasing," must be present.

How to achieve harmony, every true artist demonstrates in his work; however, in his case this is largely the result of his intuition. This, of course, is well enough for the artist; but it does not make the problem any less intricate for the student, to whom we want to explain harmony as a principle.

GREEK CARVED STONE

Museum of Fine Arts, Boston

Harmony is generally appreciated as the quality in a work of art which makes it appear as if the many component parts were related; as if there existed an affinity of the parts. Harmony, therefore, must necessarily result in a consistent expression of interior accord. It is perhaps less easily recognizable than any other æsthetic quality.

In the figures on page 164, we may study the meaning of harmony in an abstract sense, in pure design. The individual large inclosing forms are dissimilar and show very little relation to each other. However, the minor, filling forms, while they are all of different size, are all of the same kind. It is not possible to replace any one of the smaller forms with another form, taken from another inclosure, without destroying the idea of orderly relationship.

To explain in detail what it is that produces harmony in works of art, we will begin again with lines, as such, in a picture, a statue, or a building. Every artist has a certain characteristic method of linear drawing which is different from that of his fellow artists. Botticelli's outlines are reposeful,

elegant, and unmistakably different from Rubens's most animated and often exuberant lines. The individual qualities of Botticelli's lines are found persistently through all his pictures. An artist's lines may be emotional, impassioned, as in Rubens's pictures; or cool, calm, serene, and distinguished, as in the early Italian work; or, again, restrained, as in a Whistler design. A figure of Rubens transferred into a Botticelli would be grossly out of harmony and disruptive of artistic effect,

logical and effective as the figure might be in its place in Rubens's own pictures. Many interesting investigations of this kind may be made both among the old masters and among the new, and also in furniture, rugs, and sculptures,—in fact, everything possessed of form. The widely distributed work of our popular illustrators, and especially the work of our etchers, offers unending opportunity for convincing study of the personal character of the line.

A casual review of the chief exponents of the greatest

ESCRITOIRE

A piece of modern furniture conspicuous for its æsthetic qualities. The harmonious relation of the top to the feet is apparent

schools of painting will disclose the invariable presence of harmony. Every part, even the most secondary, in the work of all the great masters is in harmony with every other part of the picture, in the peculiarly individual manner in which it is carried out. The one thing which proclaims so many unoriginal pictures is their lack of harmony. They are composed, frequently, of details borrowed from a number of works of other artists,—details which, owing to their different origin, are not in accord with one another. Imagine a landscape with a Rousseau tree in the distance, sharply patterned against a clear sky, with a feathery Corot tree in the middle distance. No matter how pleasing this landscape might be to the uninitiated, it would never be convincing artistically, because it would not have a harmony of formal conception. The world of art presents just such inconsistent efforts, in the productions of the unscrupulous plagiarist. It is probably lack of time to do original thinking which sometimes forces the "commercial artist" to resort to the method of borrowing from many unrelated sources. It is the lack of time to do original thinking in commercial art which causes it to be regarded as inferior in quality. This it sometimes is; but it need not be. Again, in figure paintings where two or three unrelated types are thrown together, though they are compelled to appear together they refuse to live in the same atmosphere. Harmony of expression is found to exist in a pronounced degree in the work of the Greeks. Among modern Frenchmen, Monet and Puvis de Chavannes are excellent examples of pronounced harmony.

CHINESE VASE

Seventeenth-century carved ivory. (Metropolitan Museum, New York)

While their art is not the least alike, each one is most consistent throughout in his own method of characterization, drawing, and painting; and to imagine one collaborating in the work of the other is almost ludicrous.

Monet throughout his scintillating canvas employs a nervous technique of broken color patches which give to his work that quality of vibration for which he was willing to sacrifice other considerations. On the other hand, Puvis de Chavannes's reposeful murals are expressed in placid areas of comforting restfulness. This radical difference not only explains the marked individual note which every individual artist possesses, but it also illustrates the possibility of marked technical and formal differences occurring among different artists, provided they are consistently maintained.

A CHIPPENDALE CHAIR SHOWING GOTHIC INFLUENCE

The accompanying reproductions of two chairs and a vase demonstrate the meaning of harmony in simple terms. The student should be able from a study of these few examples to grasp the wide application of this law. The consistent use of related forms in them is so apparent as not to need further elucidation. Nature offers to the observing student similar examples everywhere. On the rounded foothills (so typical of California) we observe the round forms of the evergreen oak;

and we have another illustration in the trees growing near the jagged peaks of the Sierras and harmonious with them in form, —that is, in the firs and junipers. The beauties of Nature never seem more alluring than when one learns to recognize her generous aid in helping us to understand art principles.

Harmony of line and form such as we have been discussing are not difficult of analysis. Harmony of color, however, is perhaps more of a problem, although both its presence and its absence are readily perceived. In some color schemes, whether in painting, furniture, or dress, we are conscious of one dominant hue. This is the expression of color harmony expressed in analogies. In our consideration of colors this term will be more intensively treated. While most pictures of the older school excel in a harmony of brown, many modern painters, as we shall see, have demonstrated the possibilities of other dominant color harmonies. Our Twachtman made use of a dominant gray tonality, which he seldom lost.

A CHIPPENDALE CHAIR OF THE LATE EIGHTEENTH CENTURY

The artist feels that a picture is held together by this element of harmony, and he feels that the picture may give the impression of "falling to pieces" if it is not successful in that respect. Harmony, of course, is not necessarily based on imitation of nature, but rather on an æsthetic consideration.

However, one point must be borne in mind: that absolute sameness in itself cannot be recognized as harmony,—it must be given emphasis, must be set off by an element of occasional variation, of contrast. If every part of a picture were, in respect to line, color, and style, absolutely like every other part, the result would be monotony; and in order to avoid monotony, a distinct note of contrast must be introduced. To take one of the delightful pictures of Corot as an illustration, we may note that the woman in the center, with the red bonnet, is not there merely by accident. She was put there with a purpose. The general tonality of the picture is blue-gray-green harmony. It is bathed in quiet tones; and these are given emphasis by contrast with the little spot of vermilion so effective in the picture. Leave out this red accent, and the picture will be dull and dreary. In many portraits gay boutonnières, small bits of colorful jewelry, bright scarfs, give life to pictures which without them would be lifeless and lacking in contrast, in spite of their harmony. Naturally the effects of these things in a picture are in principle the same as in everyday life. But color is so important an element that we shall have to deal with the subject in a separate chapter, where a more ample presentation of color harmony will be found. The experienced critic is able to discover certain characteristics of contrast persistently running through all the work of any given artist.

The artist who has found himself gives to all his work a certain consistent, uniform quality which is unmistakable, no matter where we meet it. In the so-called "one-man exhibition" we can recognize at a glance the quality of consistent relationship between all the pictures which makes such exhibitions so enjoyable. This quality of relationship is no more or less than harmony. We enjoy this consistency of style in Arthur B. Davies, Redfield, Sargent, Hassam, or any other of our strong men. It is a quality seldom attained by beginners, but invariably found in a master, and it has a great deal to do with what we recognize as style. Once we become susceptible to harmony in art, we gradually learn how to look for it.

We instinctively feel the lack of artistic conviction in a dress consisting of many different kinds of goods; and we at times meet with the type of painting in which the painter has heaped together elements, magpie-like, from half a dozen different in-harmonious sources. The name given to the "crazy quilt" owes its origin to its lack of harmony. The parts of a painting, or any work of art, must appear to belong together. They must express that affinity which is one of the greatest qualities in a good work of art, contributing more than anything else to oneness of expression, to unity.

While one may be made conscious of balance and rhythm by themselves, artistic achievement in its highest expression is possible only in their unification. A work of art which has the expression of unity, of oneness, of harmonious agreement, in each and every desirable element, is bound to become ad-judged a classic in due time. The world abounds in works of art, but not all have been so inspired in every particular phase as to give one that complete satisfaction which is more readily felt than explained. Such works make us breathless. They seem to command an attitude of respect and reverence. They do not ordinarily provoke analysis, and the only thing we can do with such inspired examples is to give ourselves over to the peculiar spell they cast upon us. If it were possible here to run the gamut of the acknowledged classics in art, we should find that all breathe that perfection typical of their kind. Per-fection seems to exist in every element; and these pictures suggest also a naturalness and lack of effort equal to their other superior qualities.

It is admitted that the "great" style of painting has not often been attained since the days of Raphael or Titian, Velásquez or Rembrandt; but it is not necessarily the monu-mental in painting that gives the feeling of unity: we some-times observe it in paintings of small proportions. It must become obvious that size has little or nothing to do with unity, though it will be apparent that it is more difficult to harmo-nize large surfaces than smaller ones.

Our first feeling before any truly great painting,—as, for instance, Whistler's "Portrait of the Artist's Mother," in the Luxembourg,—aside from its marked simplicity, is that it holds together; that is to say, that every detail seems to play its part in the concert without disturbing any other part. There is no wrangling, no agitation or fuss; everything seems content in its place and satisfied with its æsthetic responsibilities. We feel about such paintings, just as we feel about great minds,

NIGHT'S OVERTURE

By Arthur B. Davies. (Minneapolis Institute of Art)

that they are perfectly at ease. They say what they have to say simply; they tell their message candidly, without stuttering. They are primarily clear in enunciation and articulation. No matter what their subject may be, no matter what their intellectual appeal, this is true of all great works of art. They seem to have been seen clearly before they were started; and we sense at once this artistic unity. Inness's "Georgia Pines" is distinctly one of his greatest works because of the unity of its expression.

We easily remember great paintings by their convincing spiritual and formal qualities. They need no explanation.

They are almost outside the pale of artistic criticism. Often they are simple in the extreme, even to the point of sternness; but they are always endowed with the telling beauty of a big and simple message. Anybody who has had the privilege of seeing Titian's "Man with the Glove," at the Louvre, or Rembrandt's "Night Watch," at Amsterdam, or Chase's "Lady with the White Shawl," at Philadelphia, or, to name a few more, Alexander's "Portrait of Walt Whitman," at the Metropolitan Museum, in New York, and Tarbell's "Mending Girl," at Boston, will know that although they were produced at different times, by different men, all seem inspired in similar ways; their appeal is inherent in the same qualities. They defy analysis, but they possess simplicity of expression in every element.

Simplicity of expression, then, has apparently a great deal to do with artistic power, and we must come to the firm belief that the agitated fussiness of the small-calibered work of art militates against its lasting effect upon our senses.

All declining periods of art have been marked by a loss of simplicity and by substitution, for the candid presentation of one essential phase, of the irritating and scattered expressions of many conflicting elements. The serenity of a Leonardo da Vinci is essentially present in a marine by Winslow Homer. We feel the same quality in two totally different subjects produced at different times. It is a certain bigness that cannot be accomplished where there is not subordination of every detail to a single predominant expression. The thrill we get from a Velásquez is one that springs from the bold and simple characterization of the outstanding qualities of his personages. We call it style, but it is the simplicity and grandeur in this style which appeal. These are the qualities which permit us to grasp the full meaning of a painting at once. Only when we can sense the entire significance of a painting in one visual attack do we seem to feel the quality of oneness.

The scattered qualities of the anecdotal schools of the last century are typical of the neglect of unity; on the other hand,

LADY WITH THE WHITE SHAWL

By William Merritt Chase. (Pennsylvania Academy of the Fine Arts)

the impressionist invariably gives us a unified expression of his subject. The difficulty of painting our great natural scenic beauties, such as Niagara or the Yosemite, lies in the fact that it seems impossible to create on the canvas the unity which we feel when the natural object is before us. What has become of that enthralling sense of the overpowering grandeur of the Grand Cañon, in the trifling depictions of some of our popular painters? It has not been realized and perhaps never will be, unless some Winslow Homer or Whistler solves the problem of artistic unity that presents itself in the great mountain architecture of our incomparable scenery. These inspiring aspects of our great country still await the day when their message will actually be carried through artistic means to everybody, not merely to those who have actually enjoyed them in reality and can thus furnish the thrill that is lacking in the picture by a spiritual revival of their own memory, their own experience.

However difficult it is to give unity to a work of art, we invariably recognize it whenever it exists. Simplicity of form will not insure its presence in a work of art, as we may readily observe in many paintings which, though simple in form, are nevertheless lacking in unity because the painter, painting merely the shell, has treated them without concentration upon the spirit. The power to paint the spirit, the soul, of an object is a gift; when it is present in a superlative degree, we call it genius.

Whenever the spirit of the subject is harmoniously supported by the formal elements, we always have great art. Modern art, perhaps, is less concerned about the spiritual than were the old masters, whose calm unity of beauty deteriorated in later ages into much sentimentality. It was logical, then, that art should become engaged in the representation of externals, without paying much tribute to the soul of a subject. In external representation we are admittedly as efficient as ever; but it is doubtful whether we always associate with it a valid psychology of the subject, such as the old masters achieved, and therefore unity has ceased to be so potent a factor in our day. It has become the tendency both of the artist and of the critic to pick out some minor element in a subject and to dwell upon it, omitting whatever major quality might demand recognition. We have rhythm, or color harmony, or vibration, or, again, light, as the sole moving force in a modernistic picture; and we are given to understand that we must not look for anything else. In the sort of painting of which this is true, the explanation is that it results from an attempt to introduce a new principle; but rarely do we get a complete thrill of utmost satisfaction from a painting of this type, such as we gain from Ter Borch's "Musician," in the British Museum, Rembrandt's "Portrait of a Polish Nobleman," in the Hermitage, at Petrograd, or the best of Sargent's portraits. These great paintings are spiritually a complete unity; they are positive, and still they leave room for suggestive interpretation. They possess perfect harmony of both spirit and form.

XIV

WHAT COLOR MEANS TO AN ARTIST

While color is a contributing factor in the appeal of architecture and sculpture, and several applied arts, it assumes a particularly important responsibility in the appeal of a painting. Since color in painting is based upon a study of color phenomena in nature, whatever principles of color use we may agree upon are equally applicable in all fields. Thus color may well be studied either through the immediate means provided by nature or in some art form produced by man. Whatever we may consider desirable as color effects in painting will inevitably be desirable in other arts, as in interior decoration, landscape gardening, architecture, and many practical arts such as ceramics and textile design. Color gives distinction to everything it touches. Wherever and whenever used with understanding, it may express a wide range of moods: gayety, even hilarity, somberness or graveness, sympathy or repugnance,—all sensations are possible of expression in color. In fact, those sensitive to color and capable of expressing it in pigments carried by either canvas, wood, silk, stone, or any other material, are able to convey very subtle differences.

Even in so brief a study of the subject as ours must, of necessity, be, we are bound to recognize not only the artist's contribution, but also the researches of the physicist and the chemist, who have materially helped to clarify the problem of the artist. We owe to the physicist our knowledge of the source of color. It was Sir Isaac Newton who demonstrated first that a beam of white light passing through a prism is broken into its constituents, which appear to the eye as definite color sensations known as red, orange, yellow, green, blue, indigo, and violet,—these colors, as in a rainbow, appearing in this order, and passing gradually into one another without abrupt transitions. Arranged in an orderly fashion in the spectral ring so well known to every art teacher, these colors have been universally regarded as the practical basis of color use. This definite color range has now become the accepted

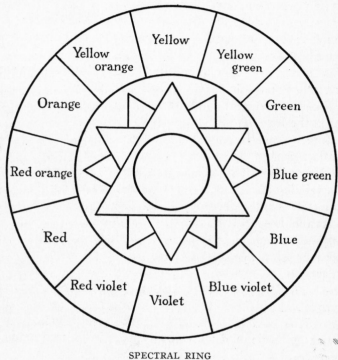

SPECTRAL RING

basis for the theory of color adopted by most artists. Following upon Newton's spectral analysis, Sir David Brewster established the idea that there are three primary colors—yellow, red, and blue—from which, in pigment form, every other known color can be mixed. This view of the three primaries has been commonly maintained by scientists and painters. Although there have been attempts to establish divergent theories, the spectral theory of Sir Isaac Newton is the one most widely recognized as the basis of a practical color theory. We are further indebted to the scientific investigations of the modern chemist, which have greatly enriched our store because many of the permanent colors which so appeal to us today are the result of his discoveries. However, the study of the origin and behavior of pigments is in itself a task involving more space than this book permits, and we must therefore omit it from our consideration. It is obviously of more importance to the artist than to the appreciator of art. One of the difficulties, aside from the very unsatisfactory use of colored charts in books, lies in the difference between the colored light of the physicist and the substitutes for them as used by the artist in the form of pigment.

Before we enter, however, upon a general discussion of the æsthetic modification of the spectral hues as represented in the color equipment of the painter, a few basic terms should be defined, in order to avoid misunderstandings. There is little misunderstanding with respect to the primary colors—yellow, red, and blue—or the binary colors,—orange, green, and violet,—the result of the pigment mixtures of the primary colors in equal parts. A mixture in pairs of the primaries and binaries gives us a group of six tertiaries: yellow-green, blue-green, blue-violet, red-violet, red-orange, and yellow-orange. All these twelve colors together are spoken of as the basic colors. It is obvious that an indefinite number of intermediaries is possible, and such subdivisions have been actually demonstrated by scientists. However, they are difficult to describe, and, for our purpose, of little importance. The fact that there are only twelve basic colors should be gratefully acknowledged by the student when he contemplates the indefinite number of modifications of these possible by various means. The basic colors as such are also spoken of as hues. They are the most intense, the most saturated, the fullest color expressions we are able to recognize.

The student should not allow himself to be confused by fashionable color designations such as henna, taupe, or beige, which, though easily recognizable by reason of their origin in natural objects, are only seasonal in their use.

The simplest modification of color for artistic effect is possible through an admixture of the basic colors with black and white, in different quantities. If white be added to a basic color, a tint is the result; on the other hand, the addition of black produces a shade. Pink, for instance, is a tint; and navy blue, the result of an admixture of basic blue with black, is a shade. Brown, although extremely common, is not a basic color but a shade of orange. If all those who resort to color for some purpose or other should learn to recognize this distinction, a very common state of confusion would be quickly eliminated.

Owing to the difference of terminology in Europe and America, another regrettable confusion exists in the nomenclature of color. Standard dictionaries in our country, as well as abroad, give to "tone," as applied to the use of color and chromatics in general, a most variable meaning, such as "the prevailing color effect of a picture, whether bright, dull, brilliant, warm, cold, or neutral in tone." "Tone" in England means the predominating color of a picture; for instance, a picture may be of a reddish or greenish tone, according to what is the controlling, prevailing hue. To many people in this country it seems that the word "tone" signifies values; that is to say, it has reference to the degree of light and dark a color possesses, irrespective of its hue or chromatic quality. The matter of value is best illustrated in the ordinary photograph, which registers values independent of color. As to brightness or brilliancy of a color, we are better able to describe it in terms of "intensity." Intensity as such may assume many degrees; ordinarily, however, colors are spoken of as appearing in full, three-fourths, one-half, or one-fourth intensity. The qualities of warmth and coldness are discussed later and are separate sensations. Shades and tints, as has been shown, are specific modifications.

The quantitative use of color, aside from its intensity or

chromatic power, is one of the problems of color which offers a test of real artistic ability. The very intense colors, like the primaries and binaries, are enjoyable only for short periods and in small quantities. What spices are in the culinary art, intense colors are in the realm of painting. Our eyes rapidly tire if fed only on very intense colors. The combination of a brown suit with an orange necktie seems agreeable; but the reverse—a brown necktie and a brilliant orange suit—would be hard to bear.

The use of color has been more daring, more pronounced, in some periods than in others. The rise of color to a very important place in our present-day art and life must impress itself upon even the most unobserving. We are at present living in an age of color, and this condition gives it added importance in art and makes an understanding of its æsthetic meaning a greater necessity than ever.

Individual endowment for the realization and use of color varies greatly with different people; in fact, we know that some people are color-blind, and entirely incapable of recognizing certain colors. Fortunately this state is relatively uncommon. It is more prevalent in men than in women. Color blindness among men, particularly with respect to red or green or both, exists in four out of one hundred men, while this handicap affects one woman in two hundred. While color blindness is always a defect, it may become an element of danger; for example, in the case of color-blind railroad engineers who cannot recognize colored signals. Happily, modern precaution has made the color-blind locomotive engineer an improbability. Men in modern civilization have become so used to having color denied them in their dress that they have come to regard it as a prerogative of women. Mere man may sport a gay necktie or aggressively hued socks; but aside from these opportunities his use of color in his external appearance is limited. It is probable, moreover, that women have always been endowed with a greater sense of color, in keeping with the needs of their sex for self-adornment.

While the disadvantage of men in the personal use of color is evident today, a review of historic styles of clothing amply demonstrates that this has not always been the case. It is not unpleasant, indeed, to contemplate the return, among civilians, of the dark-blue "cutaway" with gold buttons, the pale green vest, and the wine-colored trousers. It would be an opportunity for men which they could hardly afford to ignore. Among the chief attractions of military life, aside from the element of class privilege, have been regimental music and colorful uniforms; take away these allurements, and Mars at once becomes a very sober figure.

The very earliest known use of color, by the Egyptians and Assyrians, amounts to a genuine demonstration of a love of color for itself; and that love continues in humanity to the present day. Color has always had a very wide range of effect upon people; and we are at present treated to the offerings of very recent experimenters, who are reëmphasizing the primitive use of color which has existed throughout the world since time immemorial. The use of color to symbolize human emotions, passion, and sorrow is no new thing: it is merely a custom, based on association of ideas, which has entered into painting indirectly, and it is often brought into play. The psychological effects of colors, modified in the unlimited degree possible, are well known and have been the subject of special attention. Yellow (the symbol of the sun), the most cheerful of the primaries, expresses joy, in its absolute purity; if reduced to an impure state by the admixture of black, it suggests an impure state of mind. Hence the symbolic use of such a yellow to suggest hatred, envy. Red, the color identified with fire and blood, suggests warmth, excitement, passion, and frequently is used to denote such qualities in the representative arts. Blue, in all its soothingness and sense of distance, is lacking in aggressiveness. Of all the colors it is the most tranquil and pacifying. The binaries or secondaries naturally assume the qualities of their basic constituents. Orange combines the cheerfulness of yellow with the warmth of red; its appearance is highly stimulating whenever it occurs. In large quantities it may become irritating; when used in small quantities it often furnishes a most useful accent. Green, as the union of yellow and blue, is capable of conveying many different sensations, according to how near it is either to yellow or to blue; its effect is entirely governed by that relationship. Green, so soothing in nature, is soothing in the arts. Violet has a most peculiar charm, all its own. Its qualities are less definite than those of the other binaries. The violets, whether reddish or related to blue, always seem to rise out of the shadows; they are less personal and rather noncommittal. We may observe violet signifying the more enduring, the more constant, qualities, such as spiritual love, truth, or suffering.

Modern attempts to find analogous expressions of colors in music—an experimental effort of the musical post-impressionists—are an endeavor to represent color by a musical code. These experiments in art will scarcely affect the layman, but rather the laboratory worker in psychology, who will be much more inclined toward these abstract vagaries than the practical lover of art, who is interested in beautiful realities.

The color problem differs with every individual; and while some artists appear to express themselves with extremely little color, deriving more pleasure from form and from neutral values, or from light and dark, the great majority consider color, in combination with pattern, a most essential element in their work, whether they are easel painters, or concerned with decoration or with any other artistic indoor or outdoor problem involving adornment of surfaces. With the modern development of chemistry no known spectral hue is denied the artistic professions in their striving for original expression of color; today every color of the spectrum can be produced in permanent quality for practical use. Whether these colors will endure through centuries, it is as yet impossible to determine.

The complaint that the sympathizers with the modern schools have against the old academic schools is that they tire of the brown pictures, although these include the greatest names in the history of art. Raphael, Leonardo, Titian, Velásquez, Rubens, and Rembrandt all painted on the brown basis. Even with these great masters, while there is an occasional flaring up of color passion, it is always on the brown foundation, the brown background. That the use of color in their days was more of a formula, as compared with the freedom practiced in our day, is self-evident. The many arguments that may be made against the brown picture will, however, not set aside the fact that the warm brown as the controlling hue in a picture is as enjoyable to some as light blue or violet— the dominant hue of the moderns—is to others.

In order to understand this at present much-discussed phenomenon, one has to remember the peculiar physiological meaning of different colors. A very important fundamental factor in color enjoyment is the difference between warm colors and cold colors. The fundamental difference of appeal between these two types explains the divided allegiance of the public to the warm academic brown, on the one hand, and the cool blue-violet of the moderns, on the other. Here again, as with other artistic laws, we find in our physical experience the explanation of these differences of effect. For instance, those natural elemental forces which produce comfort and warmth are associated with red (a certain red closely resembling a reddish orange); often we think of it in connection with fire; then also we remember the setting sun, and possibly also blood, as the life element of our body. Through the power of association, then, red and any color related to red (such as brown and orange) or with a preponderance of red are sources of warmth, of comfort, of physical pleasure. On the other hand, a certain sense of coldness overcomes us in the presence of large quantities of a certain blue,— the blue of the glacier, of ice, of night,— and we have learned to associate that color with physically less comforting sensations, even with death. This physiological effect of color has become incorporated into art almost as a law; and we have grown so accustomed to it that with the introduction of impressionistic painting, it became the chief cause of the opposition of the old school to the new one. The Englishman Constable is generally spoken of as the first one to break away from the brown "sauce" when he had the revolutionary idea of wanting to paint a landscape out of doors. To us, nowadays, the idea of painting at least the preliminary studies for a landscape outdoors has become an inevitable necessity. Incidentally he discovered that shadows outdoors are blue, not brown, and also that reflections outdoors are cool, not warm; in fact, that the colors seen outdoors under an open sky appear generally affected by its cool quality. Constable is also credited with having first had the courage to paint blue and purple shadows. It matters little whether or not Constable was the first man to break away from the academic restrictions to brown; but one thing seems certain, that in 1823 he created a decided controversy by the first exhibited work representing his outdoor venture.

What symphonies of rich and luscious browns some men achieved is best indicated by the Venetians and also in the work of Rembrandt, who surpassed any painter of his day and who has never since been equaled in luminosity. We have spoken in the chapter on technical matters of the *frottis* and its generally brown or reddish tone. The nuance of brown varies with the artist, but as an undertone it seems still to be cherished even by many present-day painters. Not only the idea of warm and cold colors but the whole question of color resolves itself into a demonstrable science, of which the painter gains control as a present at birth and which scientists regard as a series of facts capable of proof in many ways.

To those moderns out of sympathy with the traditional brown of the old masters, many older pictures are much more appealing in black and white values, while others, enamored of the warm browns, seem to lose all interest in the cool values of photographic representation. The warm-brown sepia print ever satisfies one faction, while the lovers of cool grays turn to the platinum print.

There are practiced in painting, and wherever color is used, three general types of color harmonies: the monochromatic scheme; that based on the complementary opposition of different colors; and that formed by the combination of analogous colors. Monochrome pictures are those painted in many values of one color, devoid of any real color sensations and expressed merely in contrasts of light and dark, such as exist, in a high key, in a white plaster cast or, in a lower key, in the ordinary photograph. We may see examples of these monochromes in some of the galleries of Europe; they demonstrate convincingly the superiority of sculpture as a means of plastic representation. They were the consistent results of the classicistic painters who were carried away by the plaster casts of Greek statues. These "grisaille" (from the French *gris*, "gray") pictures, as they are called, painted in a scale of grays —warm or cold, greenish or reddish, in tone—today seem lamentably uninteresting because of their lack of color.

The second, the complementary, dominates in almost all the work of the older schools. The brown undertone of the Renaissance masters, supporting the rich areas of opposing blues and reds (such they mostly were), is a common feature of the older masters. We admire this in Raphael and Bellini, as well as in Murillo, and later on in Rembrandt or Reynolds, down to the Munich School and the Englishmen. From their dark foundation the complementary notes of red and blue would often rise to strike a sympathetic chord.

It is on account of its very common use in historic art that the principle of complementary colors should be understood by those who seek to appreciate art. To that end we must refer once more to the spectrum, the basis of all color theories, as indicated in the drawing on page 177. The effect of any one color can be much enhanced, by way of contrast, by the association of some other color than the one immediately preceding or following it in the spectrum. We know also that a physical experience is the basis for the regrouping of colors as complementary colors. If we look fixedly a short time at a vivid red, and, at the first feeling of optical fatigue, turn to a blank space of neutral or white tone, we behold a spot of green. If the first color looked at be violet, this spot will be a yellow, and so on. In other words, the directly opposite color in the color wheel seems to be the one which will afford the greatest amount of pleasurable relief. The skilled artist constantly gives pleasure by his intelligent application of this law, and to examine pictures—and, for that matter, all objects everywhere—for this point alone is interesting.

The most commonly used pair of complementary colors is the combination of blue-green and red. The use of large, red, warm color areas, in opposition to green or blue-green areas, in very many of the Renaissance Madonnas is too well known to need further emphasis. In landscape painting we have the delightful examples of Corot, who very cunningly and effectively introduced his red-bonneted peasant to give life to the pleasant gray-greens in his landscape. Omit the red nuance, and how dreary and lifeless those attractive landscapes would be!

We may readily observe that up to the beginning of impressionism—that is to say, the year 1870—monochromatic and complementary color schemes were used with academic regularity. With all due regard for the achievement of the old masters, our appreciation of color has become in modern times much more subjective and less academic. There has been much greater discovery of subtle color schemes in nature than there was during the so-called great periods of art, because our artists now study color in nature rather than in other works of art.

The prevailing color schemes today are not based upon opposition but rather on relation, similarity,—in short, analogies. The analogous neighborly color schemes found in the canvases of many modern masters are so removed from the darker scales of the earlier schools that it would be futile to look for any relation between them. It was largely the stimulating influence of Turner's atmospheric skies which led to the high-keyed analogies of modern schools. The foundation of golden brown, so typical of the old master, has in modern art given room to the cool, neutral, gray-violet basis of the outdoor atmosphere discovered by the impressionist. Once more a reference to the spectral chart will help to explain the strict meaning of a color analogy. Each of the three groups of binaries and tertiaries found between the primaries constitutes an analogy. Thus yellow-orange, orange, and red-orange are one; red-violet, violet, and blue-violet are another; and blue-green, green, and yellow-green constitute a third. To either of these groups one of the adjacent primaries may be safely added; and if properly harmonized through the establishment. of nearly the same value and degree of intensity, they constitute a very pleasing color relationship. Beautiful color analogies may be observed in nature in the many violets of the cineraria, the petunia, or, in lighter keys, in sweet peas; again, the gorgeous coloring of autumn foliage discloses stimulating analogies of yellow-orange, orange, and red in the leaves of maple, liquidambar, and many other trees and shrubs. The green analogies abound throughout the summer in foliage of every kind. The observing student of Nature will once more discover in her an inexhaustible storehouse of inspiration and guidance.

In painting, the clever use of beautiful analogous colors against large masses of neutral tones is Whistler's chief contribution to modern art. His delicate, sensitive arrangements of several violets, several greens, always associated with black, were never thought of in exactly the same way before his day. He expressed his æsthetic appreciation of the abstract relation of colors in purely decorative form, to the astonishment of his contemporaries.

In summing up our presentation of these fundamental methods of color associations, we should bear in mind that while any of the three may occur by themselves, they frequently appear combined. A modern canvas often will disclose the fact that the artist may begin with a monochromatic scale, to facilitate the establishment of values of light and dark; and that to this basic approach he may add some emphatic complementary scheme of yellow and violet, only to play up the yellow and violet each in a number of analogies. Obviously color will become most appealing in subtle rather than in obvious and mechanical applications. The interested student would do well to analyze color schemes wherever they are presented.

The low-keyed picture in this age of color seems to find few friends indeed. It is almost ignored. It does not seem that ours is the period of the smoke picture at all. The aristocratic dignity of a Puvis de Chavannes is taken as weakness, and other subdued color schemes are equally disregarded. It is scarcely to be expected, in view of the modern demand for high color, that the public should appreciate the noble restraint and enduring quality of the low-toned picture, for the greatest of all low-toned painters, Whistler, did not arouse any more popular interest than the man of restrained color schemes today. The picture in low tone has always to contend with the accusation of being anæmic and lifeless and remote from nature; again, the question of art is confused by those who demand imitation rather than synthetic procedure. Perhaps the lack of assertiveness in the low-keyed picture tempts us to question its conviction.

There are painters who reject a scientific knowledge of color, and who imagine that their work is full of color when it is merely full of different paints. This difference between color and mere paint is worthy of more recognition. To use a great many different paints on a canvas is hardly more than a house-painter's performance, but to gauge a number of colors so as to produce a harmony is a process involving intelligent thought. Harmony, as we have stated before, has been said to be a condition wherein a number of things have something in common, where an invisible inner accord exists. Do all paintings today really give one this feeling of an inner accord, of having a common element? This harmony—this being of the same kind, so to speak—is the strength of the low-

toned picture, and it is a very enduring quality. It is largely
the element of harmony in analogous colors—in contrast
to the color scheme based on opposing colors held together by
different qualities of relationship—which is so fascinating.

THE WHITE VASE

Although this still-life is reproduced here only in monochrome, it arouses the
idea of lively and varied color. The textural differences in the various objects
are well indicated. (From an oil painting by Hugh Breckenridge)

The degree to which an artist feels color differs with every
individual, and it is this divergence which gives to paintings
such interest. No matter what may be one's disagreement
with modern art, one fact must impress itself upon even
the most reactionary admirer of the studio brown of bygone periods: that in daring association of intense colors and

vigor of contrast many of our modern painters are achieving vital expressions which are bound to command respect and admiration.

Color may be said to epitomize the spirit of modern art; and whatever of the trivial we may sometimes observe, no matter how lax in technical execution some of our moderns may seem, in their vital color they express both daring and joy. Never before has painting been so independent in accentuating the one feature in which none of the other arts can equal it—the element of color. Many modern still-lifes are particularly excellent examples of the clarification of color in our art. The still-life offers splendid opportunities for the conscious intro-duction of daring and rival colors. The decorative and highly imaginative art of many moderns, typified by the work of Arthur B. Davies, sings with color such as we have seen only suggested before; and the virile art of Brangwyn discloses a daring juxtaposition of pure colors which defies all traditional methods. Childe Hassam, perhaps one of our most discrim-inating workers in color, owes his high standing, aside from technical qualities, undoubtedly to his highly perceptive sense of color. We are living in an age of color, and the life which modern art owes to this element will not be the least influence in fixing, ultimately, the position of present-day art in the his-tory of æsthetic expression. While, as we have seen, there are a number of very definite and demonstrable experiments the results of which have been shaped as laws to govern the use of color, it must always remain obvious that every occasion which calls for the use of color must be met by subconscious processes of selection. If it were possible to give to people that infallible sense of selection possessed by the accomplished artist, we should never be conscious that the problem exists. The best way to acquire taste in matters of color, after all, is to use color. Its use is not denied to anybody. It is not the exclusive privilege of the professional artist.

XV

TECHNICAL METHODS AND QUALITIES

An inconsiderable part of the pleasure that we gain from the contemplation of a work of art may be derived from the manner in which it is technically expressed. Artists themselves realize that the æsthetic appeal of works of art is in a large measure dependent upon niceties of technical expression for success. The layman, however, owing to his obvious lack of experience in such matters, is often in the dark. The presiding judge, a layman in art matters, at the famous Whistler-Ruskin trial is a typical illustration of this popular belief in the value of a painting as indicated by the time spent upon its execution. His poorly concealed contempt for Whistler's admission that his simple nocturne was the work of forty minutes is not shared by an artist, who knows from experience that the achievement of an artistic effect by simple means and in a short time is one of the most difficult things possible. Of course the execution of the frescoes in the Sistine Chapel was naturally a time-consuming process, as common sense will tell. But there is no direct proportion between the time expended on works of art and their artistic quality. All great works of art, irrespective of the time consumed in carrying them out, impress one with the feeling that a *maximum of expression has been attained with a minimum of means and effort*. On the other hand, the extravagant use of technical minutiæ usually has no other effect than to remind one of the person who talks much but says nothing. Even elaborate formal expression is possible with relatively simple means. A work of art is not a "stunt." Art galleries are offering many examples of pictures and statuary that undoubtedly were finished long before the artist ceased to work upon them. It is to

Rousseau, the painter of romantic landscapes, that the saying is attributed that a picture is finished when it feels finished, not when it looks finished. If the value of a work of art were determined by its production under the greatest physical difficulties, the painter standing on his head and painting with his feet would indeed be immortal.

Many people look upon the use of oil paint as the one technical means in the graphic arts capable of yielding the highest artistic results; however, oil paint is only one of the many technical media of representation in the graphic arts, each one offering possibilities the others do not offer. In fact, any given pictorial composition could be rendered in different technical methods, each one of which would have a different appeal inherent in its medium.

In graphic expression each medium yields certain qualities, just as in sculpture certain stones, woods, or metals will each give distinct character to the subject expressed in them. Encaustic, tempera, oil, water color, pastel—each has its special charm and inherent possibilities. The use of so many media in the arts is largely due to this fact, as well as to practical considerations of climate, use, and economy. The mosaic (the expression of a pictorial design in small colored stones) and the tapestry are the results of a desire for special effects and of practical considerations.

The different results in graphic art obtained by a variation of technical methods may be compared to the rendering of a musical composition by means of different instruments. As each instrument has its own mood of joy, lightness, somberness, serenity, and so forth, so the many different vehicles of representation in the graphic arts produce similar variation of quality and effect. An ordinary line drawing of Raphael's "Sistine Madonna" without any light or shade would lack depth, but it would be charming in the rhythmic flow of line. A pencil or charcoal drawing of this picture in light and shade would be rich in depth and a feeling of substance. Again, an etching of the same subject would offer still other special linear qualities.

GOBELIN TAPESTRY

Every artist must first satisfy himself as to what particular medium will best express the subject of his choice before he can proceed with its execution.

Unfortunately, of the many significant elements in art, none is treated with so little concern by the layman as the purely technical. It will not therefore surprise us to discover that seldom do artists and laymen agree upon technical qualities in a picture. The painter himself, before any other aspect is considered, persistently wishes to satisfy himself that the paint is put on the canvas in such a way as to earn his professional approval. The layman, not uncommonly, looks for the story, or content, appeal of the canvas, and the parting of the way takes place at this point. If artists could convince laymen of the æsthetic pleasures inherent in technical processes, they would remove a great stumblingblock in the path of appreciation. We cannot blame the painter for his interest in technique, and we must also admit that the layman deserves sympathy, for the reason that perception of technical excellence is in a measure dependent upon technical experience, which the latter does not have.

Since painting is very much like writing, in that it differs vastly with individuals, it is no wonder that the method of disposing the pigment upon the canvas presents a problem in which a uniform method must not be expected. We find in all the arts a great variety of technical usages which add much to their enjoyment. In the days when painting was largely an imitative effort, the method of technique was often concealed, care being invariably taken by the artist not to disclose his technical procedure, for fear of spoiling the illusion of his purely imitative handiwork. That attitude still governs the practices of some painters of the present day, who are inclined, like their predecessors, to let their work be carried by the content alone, without any added attraction resulting from their skill in handling their material. Paintings which follow this method are apt to be very dull. As the æsthetic possibilities of painting were discovered, painters gradually grew to appreciate the difference between the skillful and the unskillful, the easy and the difficult, the interesting and the uninteresting, the matter-of-fact and the æsthetically satisfactory. Out of this knowledge has evolved the technical ideal: a maximum of effect and expression with a minimum of effort and material.

PERSIAN TILE

Metropolitan Museum of Art

The layman is, on the whole, convinced that the most difficult feat is so to execute a painting as to destroy all evidence of how it is done, and accordingly he admires immensely paintings and statuary resembling in smoothness of finish, let us say, an oilcloth. The man in the street fortifies himself behind the belief that this highly polished, smooth finish was the manner of the great masters, pointing with pride to Raphael's Madonnas and Leonardo's smiling ladies and the great number of painters of polished surfaces, without realizing that they have long since been surpassed in freshness of execution, beauty of surface, and spontaneity of method. While it is true that no work of art like Leonardo's "Mona Lisa" has ever appeared since his day, we ought not to forget that it is her subtle smile, her calm serenity, which are so compelling, and that her appeal is not due solely to the very cautious method of painting employed. Painting has greatly improved since then in representing texture, the differing qualities of different surfaces. The faces of the Madonnas of our Gari Melchers and Abbott Thayer are spiritually as exhaustive studies as those of many of the older masters, but they possess in addition a certain added charm of life, of vitality, which the older painters did not attain. The older methods of painting were, generally speaking, thin, though not invariably so, as is evidenced by certain exceptional painters, such as Rembrandt in his painting of the "Man with the Helmet," upon which paint has been loaded. It was not necessary to resort to any heavy or opaque painting to represent the indoor subjects, generally dark in tone. The necessity for a technical change in that direction did not develop until the problem of outdoor painting forced the painters into a heavier application of paint, which on the whole seems to the laymen to indicate a technically inferior method and a less accomplished painter. When Constable and his French followers, the Barbizon men, went outdoors, the necessity for rapid work did not allow the careful gauging of the quantity of paint,—to the detriment, in the popular eye, of the appearance of their canvases.

This laid the foundation for the discoveries of the seventies, —for what is now spoken of as impressionistic painting, an art which has as much sound technical basis as it has æsthetic interest. Before the days of Monet the generally adopted method of painting was to lay paint upon the canvas, by means of brushing in downward strokes, mostly executed in a slightly slanting way from the upper left toward the lower right. Painting had to be executed in that manner, and to do anything else meant an infraction of the rules of the academies. The rule was based on the custom of using the right hand to work with and on a regard for the law of gravity, and it was also for the convenience of the painter, that he might see what he was doing.

FIVE O'CLOCK JUNE

A commonplace subject presented in a fascinating technique. An excellent example of impressionism in content and treatment. (From the oil painting by Robert Spencer)

The light indoors, in a studio, is a concentrated light, owing to its passing through a window opening; outdoor light is available from every angle. The rule is as arbitrary as the academic and antiquated rule that the light in a picture must fall into it from the upper left-hand corner; and this arises from the fact that the light falls that way upon the canvas of the painter, who, working with the right hand, must have his light from the left in order to see what he is about. To realize how arbitrary these rules are, one has only to think of the left-handed painter. To say that one way is right and that there is no other is not consistent with the facts and is preventive of progress.

The impressionistic painter, working largely out of doors, threw most studio conventions to the wind. He put his paint on to suit his own needs, often very heavily in order to get body; and, in his search for light and for expression of texture, violated many of the old sacred rules of the studio. Working in a high key, mostly in tints, he had to use large quantities of white paint. He was at first promptly rejected, not only by the public but also by artists; but now, after some forty years, we acknowledge that the impressionistic method contributes the most significant technical advance of the last century. A greater change yet came, however, with the neoimpressionistic painter and his scientific way of achieving luminosity. Nevertheless, our modern exhibitions owe much of their appeal to the very general use of this latest method, although in its application it is often modified by academic methods.

The old academic method of painting was one of unbroken surface, though a colored undertone was often permitted to make itself felt throughout the canvas. This method of employing an undertone is still in vogue, and probably always will be, since it is the foundation of individual expression, through the great varieties of tone it makes possible and also by reason of the technical durability it gives to a picture. It is interesting to study pictures and to see what undertone is used. The undertone is a first rub-in (called by the French *frottis*) of some color,—generally warm, such as reddish or greenish brown,—very thinly applied, into which, while it is still wet, the final heavy color is put. To put the final expression into the wet *frottis* has always been considered a technical accomplishment of the first order. Only the elect, like Velásquez, achieved it, and the paintings produced in this manner unquestionably include many of the greatest. Into a

GENERAL HENRY KNOX

A splendid technical performance which only the study of the original in the Boston Museum of Fine Arts can entirely reveal. (Painted by Gilbert Stuart)

wet, rich undertone of a sympathetic brown a few lighter and darker tones are set, with surety of touch and keenness of perception. Many of Duveneck's and Chase's canvases have this directness and simplicity derived from putting the final painting immediately and broadly into a wet and sympathetic underpainting. Duveneck's "Whistling Boy," among others, is a good example of this method, though all his work is easily recognizable by the same quality. Even in landscape, some of the very greatest paintings are interesting for the same manner, as Inness's "Coming Storm," in the Buffalo Fine Arts Academy, will prove to even a layman. Such directness, such swiftness and energetic method, are enjoyable in the extreme. In spite of its apparent completeness, this was perhaps the work of an hour, and technically it looks the part. The apparent sense of ease with which such works are executed conveys to the beholder a pleasant feeling that the artist himself enjoyed the spontaneous use of his brush.

This direct method of starting a picture in a neutral color in different values—that is to say, expressing it in light and dark, irrespective of the actual color—has many advantages, and the best works produced by this method are as fine as any resulting from other methods, past or present. One should, however, discriminate between the spontaneously painted picture—where underpainting and overpainting are done in one sitting, where everything is risked in one bold effort—and the other type, in which the *frottis* is painted at one time and allowed to dry, and the picture then finished on a number of consecutive occasions. Our own Sargent is a past master of the first method, and some of his best canvases are painted in a now-or-never spirit, the excellence of which we rarely meet. It is this technical swiftness and facility in which Sargent has a particular skill and in which he at times equals even Velásquez. At its best, this method of apparent ease is convincing by reason of its freedom from hesitation and fumbling.

After the thin, brown underpainting we have the impressionist, searching for light, and after him the neoimpressionist (whom we abandoned in our discussion), searching for more light. The light palette, brilliant with color, was not sufficient for the neoimpressionist: he wanted the utmost in brilliancy and sparkle. Here, fortunately, science came to the rescue. Having become interested in the problem of the painter who

paints in the open air,—the plein-airist,—the scientist pointed
out to him that small quantities of different colors put alongside each other would at a distance appear like the direct mixture of two made on the palette. For instance, small particles
of red and yellow, if they are placed close together in an alter-
nate series, will give us orange; yellow and blue so arranged

THE RIVER IN WINTER

Oil painting by Edward Willis Redfield

will give us green; and so forth. The principle here illustrated
applies to all colors resulting from the methods of color mixture explained in the chapter on color.

This scientific rediscovery stimulated artists to technical
activities which surprised the public to a greater degree than
anything had before. These dotted, or stippled, pictures upset
all time-honored convictions, and the close examination of pic-

tures could no longer be enjoyed. However, neoimpressionism is still with us, and we have grown to like it. The work of Hassam, one of the outstanding figures in modern American art, is as popular as the paintings of the older schools, and Metcalf's night pictures awaken poetic sentiments in many. Ochtman's charming landscapes, and even those delightful quarries of our very versatile Daniel Garber, show the symptoms of neoimpressionistic influence. Our modern art is dominated by it because our art in America is so largely the art of outdoors, the art of the landscape painter.

No matter what the particular method of the period has been, in one regard painters have always agreed: this is in the desire to use whatever may be their personal methods to express themselves easily and skillfully, with grace and charm. We find that endeavor always, no matter how different the technique.

The question of technical quality is naturally governed by the effect desired, plus individual qualities, and any art exhibition will disclose as many methods as there are artists. One of the most acutely interesting and competent of present-day painters in a technical sense is our own Redfield. There is a considerable degree of romantic appeal in his work, and in its straightforward method of painting it is almost in a class by itself. He presents the interesting phenomenon of a most heavily painted picture which invites close inspection and which reveals a fascinating technical quality almost sculptural in effect. One's admiration grows for the painter of these suggestive fragments of nature, largely because the semiplastic handling of the paint seems most carefully considered in each stroke, with a full feeling of the responsibility of making it tell not only constructively but by enlivening the surface of the painting, by catching light and throwing shadows. Redfield's art is representative of that of many modern Americans who fascinate us by the technical skill and animation of their most original work. One feels that here paint causes pleasurable sensations not experienced in academic work. Although the suppressed emotionalism of Whistler's painting is inimitable and vexatious, it seems almost lifeless today alongside of the paintings of Symons, Lie, Beal, Bellows, Waugh, and others. After some reflection about this technical procedure among the moderns, one cannot but come to the conclusion that it is just because of the possibility of using paint in this live way

COMING OF THE LINE STORM

Unusual brilliancy and force of execution characterize this painting. (By Frederick Judd Waugh)

that painting really gains in interest. Pictures painted in an abstract, meaningless style will certainly arouse no interest for their technical qualities. A consideration of paintings of this sort must make the fact clear to the layman that the handwriting of a painter is one of his most valuable assets. To be sure, the catchy legerdemain performances of certain artists are often as quick in captivating one's eye as they are in boring one's intellect. They are often merely skill and nothing more. Mere skill, of course, in any art is hardly enough, though it must be the support of the artist in facilitating the transmission of an idea to the canvas. The *alla prima* methods of stenographic painting often profess to have as an ideal the fluent and direct methods of Velásquez or Franz Hals. Some artists do not realize that much of their wild dash is nothing more than a physical stunt, lacking in idea, mood, and observation. The present-day leaders in the field of portrait painting—artists like Sargent, Hopkinson, Cecilia Beaux, or Orpen in England— never allow one to stop with an enjoyment of mere beauty of paint, but they carry one simultaneously into a realization of the psychological depths of their sitters.

"Style" is often defined as the individual element in technique; and while the word should not be so restricted in application, it does include in its meaning this personal quality. It is, then, the personal quality in technique that gives to the work of a painter its individuality. Whatever technical qualities we may observe in painting, analogous qualities are recognizable in sculpture, literature, music, and the other arts.

XVI

THE NUDE IN GREEK AND MODERN ART

The achievement of Greek art culminated in the glorious creations of the sculptors; it is here that we find the fullest expression of the Greek ideal of perfection, expressed in terms of the human figure. The museums of the world abound in classic sculpture, both in suggestive fragments and in complete and eloquent original statues. Although the copies are replicas in plaster of Paris, devoid of the qualities of marble and bronze, they nevertheless readily convince those of us who are deprived of the originals, that the Greek artist fully understood the nobility of the human figure.

The comment is not infrequently made that the classic point of view is not indicated always in modern figural art; that it is generally lacking in painting, and that the nudes in the art of today have not much in common with the ideal of Greek sculpture expressed in abstract beauty, noble proportions, pureness of line, and rhythm of form. To a Greek sculptor, a human body was the most expressive symbol of nature, the very noblest product of creation. Even though Greek statues and portraits sometimes bear the names of individuals, their abstract beauty is so compelling as to make them independent of specific names for their artistic appeal. More often these noble forms express beauty abstractly: they are an idealized expression of the perfect human specimen, which probably did not then and does not now in reality exist. The statues of the Greeks, whether of deity or human subject, possessed in common certain qualities of beauty which assumed the character of an artistic convention, and these qualities have resulted in what we call classic style.

Indubitably a Greek statue was not a faithful reproduction of one particular figure, as if cast from life, but was rather the result of the observation of a great many models, all inspiring in different ways, in form or proportion. The qualities of classic statues have been analyzed by artists and archæologists, and a canon of beauty has been laid down as representing the fundamental artistic requirements of the human proportions in art. Any artist may have access to this table of measurement nowadays; it is the common property of all workers in the arts. And even so, modern nudes, in sculpture or in painting, are admittedly not as excellent as the classic figures.

In order to understand the high order of work of the Greek sculptor, we must learn to see that the idea of photographically correct physical representation, or rather realistic imitation, never guided him in his work.

The study of the well-known statue on page 207 illustrates, in the main, the concepts under which the Greek sculptor approached his problem. We are at once conscious that the Greek artist never succumbed to the temptation of deceiving anyone into thinking that his handiwork was actually the representation of a living being. Most emphatically he created a work of art based upon the human figure, to emphasize his keen feeling for beautiful form. In this classic statue we see Electra and Orestes in friendly conversation, the former clad in the light and typical garment of the Greek, the other devoid of any clothing. The clothed figure of Electra emphasizes the undraped body of the Apollonian Orestes. The conversational tone of the scene between the two figures is expressed in the general attitude of the two. The pose is lifelike but not absolutely an imitation of life. In fact, the supports between the hanging arm and right leg, and again between the two figures, make us conscious of the processes of sculpture. The general proportions are idealistic; that is to say, more symmetrical, more harmonious, more rhythmic, than those which nature commonly gives to human beings. The entire treatment of form throughout is directed toward perfection, not imperfec-

ELECTRA AND ORESTES
Naples Museum

tion; no opportunity was overlooked by the artist to take hold of a natural suggestion of beauty and carry it on to utmost perfection. The figure of Electra has lost none of its beauty under the graceful drapery of her loosely fitting gown; in fact, the gown seems to accentuate the flow of form everywhere, without any loss of structural feeling in this figure. Thus the Greek sculptor who charmed his contemporaries delights us today, and will no doubt afford delight for all time. Perhaps the sculptor of the past, if he had had at his disposal the technical facilities of the modern age, might have been tempted to imitate with the idea of absolute deception. However, imitation either of form or of color never tempted him; yet artists and lay public alike admire the beauty of the classic sculpture.

The individual model, posing for such a figure, became subordinated to the artist's conception of good form, line, and proportion. Every feature shows the conscious formality of such art: the treatment of the hair and the other minor details show the same conventional handling as the larger forms. The ears in a Greek statue were always beautifully proportioned and well attached; they did not express so much an individual ear as an ideal ear, made up of all the qualities of the most perfect ears that could be observed among many individuals. The hands, the feet, were shaped as Nature sometimes produced them; but she produced them seldom thus, and only in her favorite children. But what has remained of this artistic conception of the human form in the subsequent art periods down to the present day? We observe little of it between the disintegration of the Roman Empire and the Renaissance, the intervening periods offering as a rule the most primitive renderings of human form. The Renaissance, again, gave us many noble expressions of undraped human forms, which a prejudiced world hesitates to receive on the same basis as the ancient classics.

However, what wealth of beautiful and significant form there is in Michelangelo's carved marble "Slave," now in the Louvre! Originally designed to form a part of the tomb of

SLAVE

By Michelangelo

Julius the Second in Rome, but never put into place because of the fact that the project was abandoned, this expressive figure has lost none of its artistic significance even in its present detached location. A major line of movement shaped like the letter *S* runs through this composition, contributing the rhythmic motive used in many of Michelangelo's dynamic figures. The suffering of a miserable human being appears to have resolved itself into formal beauty. It is not the contortion of a body racked with pain, but rather the spiritual expression of suffering of the noblest being made by the Creator. It is idealism of a very high order based upon a realistic subject.

With the northward movement of art the human form, owing to climatic conditions and also to other causes, apparently became less familiar to artists and more and more obscured, owing to the artist's lack of everyday opportunities for the study of the nude,—opportunities which the Greek sculptors enjoyed so largely in their gymnasia. It is interesting to speculate as to what would be the artistic result if figural art should become the heritage of a people living in the tropics, rather than of a Northern people obscured by clothing. The artist of the North found himself obliged to resort to the artificialities of the studio model, and this limited opportunity for the study of the human figure may be one of the causes of the many disappointing efforts present-day sculptors and painters present to their public. In many instances, also, their productions are but imitative repetitions; too seldom are they translations or interpretations. Furthermore, many are very frank in their outright attempt to be suggestive and even sensual. Certain modern French painters produced many nudes at one time universally recognized as the "American saloon nude." Water will always find its level, and the saloon nude, conceived in the saloon spirit, never could rise to higher appeal, free from the base atmosphere of its existence. Many such pictures must be called indecent in content, and one cannot but feel astonished at the frankness of their authors. No other potentialities of appeal—and there are often some formal elements of beauty—in these pictures have any chance to assert themselves. Far too many modern nudes impress one as mere literal imitations of a particular individual model, sometimes to an embarrassing degree of photographic physical resemblance.

No doubt it is very tempting, owing to the modern highly perfected technical means of deception in the painter's and sculptor's media, to yield to a desire to imitate. The worker in three dimensions, the sculptor in marble, knows that nobody

SACRED AND PROFANE LOVE
By Titian. (Borghese Gallery, Rome)

will take his creation for the real; but the painter, although—in the physical sense—he is deprived of the third dimension in his work, often attempts the near-photographic. It will readily be seen that, as with other subjects in art, the most satisfactory results might be obtained by relying upon a well-trained memory, following the method of Böcklin and other masters. Such sea-roving creatures as Böcklin invented could never be found in the flesh, and that reason alone forced him to proceed with absolute independence of the model. Many of the greatest figure-painters must undoubtedly have created their work in this indirect way. How otherwise could many Renaissance painters have painted their large canvases of human figures with such remarkable spontaneousness and ease? Results such as they achieved cannot be accomplished in the presence of models or, directly, from smaller sketches and studies: they are the result of feeling, not of seeing. The elevating qualities indicated in Titian's so-called "Sacred and Profane Love," one of his most famous works, are probably the result of this method. The nude in this figure is most beautiful in the harmony and linear rhythm of the body. Once more, beautiful form as created by the artist transcends nature in its consistent manifestation of beauty throughout this rich composition.

Since the undraped figure is not so common a sight with us as it was in the classic periods, that consideration alone makes the position of the modern painter of figures more difficult; and since social and moral prejudices do not allow him access to the best types, in reality he should more and more be satisfied with a conventional form. He ought to appeal, above all, to our artistic senses rather than to the physical instincts.

The revival of the classic ideal in France under the Empire found expression in the exquisite linear draftsmanship of Ingres, whose "La Source," in the Louvre, is considered a convincing demonstration of the lasting qualities of classic art as expressed in modern terms. Ingres undoubtedly endeavored to accomplish in terms of paint what the Greeks expressed in the plastic media. If we may trust public opinion in this instance, he achieved a masterpiece. In the very modern sense, his work is perhaps not to be regarded as a painting, in the meaning of Velásquez or Rembrandt; but none will question the purity of form, simplicity, and freedom from imperfection of this appealing picture.

Essentially, the difficulty today with many painters and sculptors, in using the human form, is that they are unable to free themselves of the influence of the individual before them. It is here, again, as with the landscape painter of immature attitude: he copies directly, clinging to the belief that his salvation lies in the faithfulness of his adherence to the fact. In a nude executed according to this plan the result becomes doubly unsatisfactory, because the indelicate exposure of a

physical characteristics of an individual. It was this phys-
icalness in painting which moved the Puritan forefathers to
turn against art.   In their indignation against what they perceived to be immoral they condemned all art and deprived
themselves stoically of æsthetic pleasure.   There is something

DANCER AND GAZELLES
By Paul Manship

repulsive to many about the vulgarity of the photographic
nude that militates against the fair treatment of the whole
problem of the nude in the hands of the public. The nude
which has a definite artistic message does not stoop to the
voluptuous. Its claim is not physical, but based on rhythmic
contours, good proportion and spacing within the frame, and
pure color and tonal qualities.

One of the very finest examples of modern art, one that is

beyond all question free from the suggestive and full of the logic of its milieu, is Millet's "Goose Girl," in a gallery at Bordeaux, France. Here we see the budding form of a country girl relinquishing her task of leading the village flock of geese, and quietly dipping into the shallow waters of a brook. Whether she was ever observed in actuality by the artist or not we do not know; but if we knew something of Millet's methods, we may be sure that the picture was largely the result of a retentive and constructive mind. In any case, the whole work is so thoroughly convincing that nothing but complete æsthetic satisfaction will result from a contemplation of this, one of Millet's best-known masterpieces.

The question of morality and art today has assumed a very acute aspect. Human nature remains unchanged, but at the present time we have developed frankness in dealing with matters fundamental to morality. We have cause to believe that we are not less moral than our predecessors were. Clandestine practice has been superseded by out-in-the-open frankness. Which is better?

Idealization, we have learned, is not one of the qualities accepted as essential in art among a great many of the radical modernists; but while one may rarely be offended by the candid realism of a still-life or a landscape, the insistent vulgarity of some modern nudes in art is scarcely reconcilable with æsthetic demands. We may be indebted to modern tendencies for much wholesome agitation; but in the artistic treatment of the human form we are farther away from the classic ideal than in any other subject in art, and we have not yet proved that we can find a satisfactory substitute for that ideal.

Our leading sculptors show a much better understanding of the problem than our painters, perhaps partly because in their medium the painters have not before them the examples of the Greek ideal. Sculptors such as Taft, Aitken, Longman, Whitney, and Manship are worthily upholding the classic ideal in dealing with the nude human figure, which will always remain the finest symbol of æsthetic perfection.

XVII

THE ECONOMIC SIDE OF ART—ART PATRONAGE

In order that the student may gain a proper perspective of the economic and social factors which influence modern art, he must always remember that in the earliest historic periods in Egypt the artist was not honored as he came to be in Greece, in the Renaissance, and eventually in modern society. He was ordinarily one of the working class in Egypt; the artist was lost in the house painter or decorator, the mason or builder, the craftsman generally. The young man or woman of today, contemplating a career in art, would do well to serve a craftsman apprenticeship, in which he would gain a respect for the value of sound workmanship and labor.

The practice of today of placing speculative values on such art products as easel pictures is the cause of much discontent among craftsmen, who rightly feel that the evaluation of their product is based only on its material worth, with no allowance for its beauty. Our materialistic age has so emphasized the importance of money as a criterion that the modern craftsman no longer finds his reward in part in that happiness which comes from the creating of beautiful objects.

In the days of Phidias, art was largely a concern of the state; today, with us in America, it is governed largely by public interest and approval. While in the later periods in the development of European art practical support was furnished exclusively by the dominant religious and political organizations, such as the Church and the aristocracy, the course of art here in America clearly demonstrates how in a democratic country the life and existence of art may well depend entirely upon the broadest popular support, and not merely upon the interest of the well-to-do or socially prominent. Patronage of art in that sense has never been confined in this country to any small, select group of interests centralized in the Church, the government, or the moneyed aristocracy, and it is this fact that raises one's hopes to expect more of the art of our country in the future than of that of European countries, where conditions in this respect have suffered little modification since early times.

During the greater part of the Renaissance the Church was practically the sole art patron; artists looked to the Church for support, and this one-sided patronage naturally produced a very one-sided art, reflecting only one definite phase of civilization. We are tempted to believe that artists took no interest in the many suggestions which must undoubtedly have come to them in those days from the many other aspects of life; one finds but scattered evidences that their Italy was populated by anything but Madonnas and saints. This concentration upon one subject without question produced the flower of religious paintings, but it demonstrates also the limitations resulting from exclusive patronage.

Eventually, with the decline of the influence of the Church, the worldly nobles, like the Medici and other moneyed aristocrats, assumed the responsibility of caring for the promotion of artistic aims, either for æsthetic gratification or for purely selfish purposes of dynastic self-glorification. We find during the sixteenth and seventeenth centuries, throughout many European countries, that art was put to the service of the aristocracy, to help perpetuate their reign by preserving the dazzling, awe-inspiring phases of their more or less artificial existence. The masses had to be impressed with the wealth, the power, and the glory of the reigning families if they were to be kept in servile obedience. A true art of the common people in those days did not exist. The early Dutch, independent in so many ways, had far less of this subservient attitude toward religious and political institutions than the other peoples of that time. Art history shows, through the productions of those independent workers, very consistently and gradually, the slipping away of the arts from the grasp of hereditary authority represented by either Church or State.

So today only the most paternal government openly dares to prescribe subjects for the pictures of its State-supported students, although in some countries encouragement is offered young artists in the shape of commissions to execute expressions of official art; that is, expressions which will help to perpetuate the systems in power and to make more secure existing political institutions. Even today we still officially glorify war, rather than peace, through the medium of art.

In the case of the churches of today, decline in art patronage is very evident, and it is to be regretted, both for the sake of the churches and for the sake of the artists. The religious painter in the old sense exists no more: there are no longer produced the religious paintings in the manner of the old masters, dealing with the Madonna or with the rewards for the good and the penalties for the wicked. And this decline is no indication that we are less religious than our forefathers. It is just that the whole system of patronage has changed, and the change presents, here in America, particularly in relation to the churches, some most interesting and novel phases. Our modern churches are often very sober because their congregations fail to find exaltation in their houses of worship, without realizing that a feeling of detachment from the outer world is not stimulated by coarse architecture badly composed, stained-glass windows, and an artistically poor ensemble in general.

The value of art as a stimulant to introspection is expressed by an art-loving pastor, Van Ogden Vogt, in the preface to his book "Art and Religion." "To artists and lovers of the beautiful, I want to speak my definite expectation of a time soon to come again when patrons of the arts will see in the religious institution an incomparable opportunity for the most persuasive influence of beauty upon the people. Every church building in village or city should itself be a noble work of art. And the arts have each a proper place in the fostering of the su-

preme experience of worship." Thus the churches will symboli-
cally express the human ideal of perfection through recourse
to the arts.

The most significant factor today in patronage is the growing independence of the modern artist, who often wants to
serve only himself. When, as in the past, little was done except
by commission, a spirit of self-satisfaction and loss of individuality were likely to develop, while in our modern age the artist's thoughts are much less diverted from his work by the
bias of the interested patron. Modern artists produce, first of
all, to satisfy themselves, to realize their own ideal, irrespective of the objective use and application of the work. Undoubtedly the modern spirit in art owes much to its freedom
from official patronage. The pathfinders, the innovators, in
modern art often dare to follow their convictions only on account of this very freedom from official patronage.

In the earlier days of American civilization we manifested
little concern for the home production in art; in fact, we most
consistently preferred art made abroad, and it was not always
the best, either, that crossed the Atlantic. There was perhaps
little to choose from at home, but the few artists here were
early made conscious that there was no hope for them in this
great country. This state of affairs continued for a long
time, even into the middle of the last century, when we had
already produced excellent artists like Stuart and Inness,
whose work compared favorably with that of their popular
European contemporaries. The only course open to artists
of earlier days was to save sufficient means to enable them
to reside in countries where governments and other agencies were more kindly disposed toward them and where the
standing of artists was socially higher than at home. Even
today our very rapidly increasing art patronage is still partly
motivated by a desire for something we observe in the possession of other nations rather than by our acknowledgment of
the responsibilities of the public toward the artist.

In our very earliest days of American art, in colonial days, the historians tell us of our painters' having to turn to house decorating and painting of signs for tradesmen's shops in order to eke out a living. Since Watteau and others, even Titian, did similar things, no odium should be attached to their having done so. Conditions generally were no different in our pioneer days from what they had been in earlier periods abroad. Slowly we have changed, and at present an interest in art is developing in this country which promises well for the future of American art and the enrichment of our lives.

ALBRIGHT ART GALLERY, BUFFALO

It is instructive and interesting to compare present-day methods of support abroad with those in the United States. Abroad, under the paternal system, the government officially controls the channels through which the artist receives his financial and social encouragement; and the latter is by no means less welcome to him than the former. The craving for social prestige in the past deprived America of the presence of some very capable American-born artists who preferred to live in foreign countries where honors, decorations, titles, and like distinctions give the artist a social standing which he cannot hope to attain at home. Whatever such distinctions may be worth, the case of any American artist residing abroad affords ample illustration of the difference between continental and American methods of treatment of artists. Until recently the American artist abroad, if he was at all successful, usually possessed a kite tail of honors and decorations; on the other hand, many of those who stayed at home were quite without such decorations, medals, honorary offices, degrees, largely because such things are not considered essential in a democracy. Unfortunately, the public is more likely to recognize the artist who has a lengthy biography. But, after all, the relative merit of the American artist residing abroad and of the one who casts his lot with his native land is not measured in terms of decorations.

Moreover, we are now gradually supplying in the United States the means of formal recognition of artists, and it appears that we may be going to rival Europe in the establishment of monetary prizes and awards for them. Ours do not as yet mean quite as much internationally as the foreign emoluments, but eventually time and tradition will supply the dignity necessary for their effect.

In our country it is the generous attitude of the private citizen which has furnished the most effective means for the cultivation of the fine arts. That is to say, with us it is the private citizen of small as well as of large means who has contributed the money necessary for the support of the artistic professions. We may write about art and profess to be interested in it, but the only means by which the growth of art can be measured is by the relative amount of money put at its disposal. The world has seen some very interesting examples of the power of patronage in promoting art. Money alone without national professional ability for artistic production will not, of course, suffice; but after the artistic capacity of a people has been demonstrated, the thing most necessary is financial support. The establishment and success of Munich as an art center were due entirely to the lavish endowment of artistic enterprises by a Bavarian king, who had to provide special attractions, in the promotion of his scheme for the development of his capital, on account of the fact that rival cities offered more favorable climatic conditions. Art in Munich always flourished, though in rather a raw climate, because of lavish patronage. The one similar American example is that of Pittsburgh, where, under industrial conditions, the munificence of one citizen has been responsible for the most important art exhibitions on the American continent. Surely there are in the United

THE MINNEAPOLIS INSTITUTE OF ARTS

States other cities than Pittsburgh destined through cultural tradition, artistic interest, and climatic conditions to be leaders in art. But, strangely enough, it is the liberal interest of one man which has provided for Pittsburgh the distinction of holding the most important artistic event in the United States, the biennial international exhibitions of the Carnegie Institute.

The commanding artistic standing of the French is the result of the persistently kindly and generous attitude of that nation toward its artists. No other people has so liberally and tactfully looked after the needs and interests of the artistic professions as have the French, and the national benefits derived have surely paid for the policy. France has set the example and furnished the method of practical promotion of art which has become the guiding rule for many of the modern countries. We here in America have adopted in various ways the methods of the French, and our system of art patronage is brought over directly from Paris, the modern Mecca of American artists. "Les amis d'art," emulated by the "Friends of American Art" at Chicago, and societies of similar names elsewhere, have been of great encouragement to the profession, and a cultural impetus in many communities.

While organized interest in art in this country goes back as far as 1804,—to the foundation of the Pennsylvania Academy of Fine Arts,—the more solid support of art was caused by the great American expositions. The year 1876, the year of the Centennial Exposition at Philadelphia, is generally counted as the turning-point which marks the awakening of a national consciousness of American art. Again, the Chicago Exposition in 1893 greatly stimulated the art of the Middle West. In St. Louis in 1904, and in San Francisco and San Diego in 1915, the American public reveled in the pride of having discovered a native American art. Since the days of Philadelphia we have undoubtedly made enormous strides in art, and the very rapid growth in the United States of publicly supported institutions and societies devoted to art is astonishing. In 1882 a report on art education prepared by the United States government points out thirty museums existing at that time, and the first volume of the *American Art Annual*, published in 1898, enumerates forty-one. Since then the increase has been surprising, so that we have at present in this country about eighty art museums, nearly two hundred and fifty art schools, and other art organizations rapidly approaching the thousand mark. We learn further, from the same source, that the first American museum to be devoted wholly to art was the Wadsworth Athenæum, at Hartford, opened in 1842, to which the Morgan Memorial has been added within recent years. Of course, the names of our famous older art galleries are familiar to all—

the Corcoran Art Gallery at Washington, the Metropolitan Museum at New York, the Boston Museum of Fine Arts, and the Chicago Institute of Art. But it is interesting to learn of the establishment of many new museums. Among these are the Watson Memorial at Rochester, dedicated in December, 1913, and the Los Angeles Museum, opened in 1914. The magnificent building of the Minneapolis Institute of Arts is

ALFRED O. DESHONG MEMORIAL ART GALLERY, CHESTER, PENNSYLVANIA

partly completed, and an important art museum has been recently opened at Cleveland. Smaller galleries, recently dedicated, include that at Stanford University, in California, and the Deshong Memorial, at Chester, Pennsylvania. Recent public bequests have provided for the Peter A. Gross Gallery, at Muhlenberg College, Allentown, Pennsylvania; the Franklin Simmons Museum, at Portland, Maine; the California Palace of the Legion of Honor at San Francisco; and the H. H. Huntington Gallery, at Pasadena. All this generosity is gratifying and encouraging. Most of these museums are permanent structures and architecturally of very great beauty, and their collections will be diversified and representative.

The good that some of these institutions have accomplished for the public is very far-reaching. A new art museum, the Butler Art Institute, at Youngstown, Ohio, displays over the entrance the legend "Pro bono publico." This concern "for the public good" is reflected in many other of our recent gifts and endowments. Moreover, there is an increasing belief, even among foreigners, that the activities of our art institutions are much more progressive and truly useful than similar institutions abroad. They are not confined merely to the regular exhibitions, composed of the permanently owned works, and open to the public at little or no cost, but are broadened by very liberal courses of lectures, public instruction to young and old, and education generally, reaching in a truly democratic way far into the hearts of all classes of people. The activities of these institutions are carried into remote districts; and, in fact, in many instances even the smallest communities have an art club.

While much of our present art enthusiasm is indiscriminate, it shows what we may eventually expect in permanent values if the standards of appreciation continue to rise. The most promising feature of the art situation is the turning of our industrially acquired wealth toward cultural institutions. This started with general university endowments, and has gradually singled out special professions like medicine or law and, increasingly, the arts.

To give the student a significant and suggestive idea of the magnitude of monetary gifts for the support and encouragement of various kinds of art activities, one need merely refer to the *American Art Annual* of 1917. Here it is reported that the gifts and bequests of the preceding year comprise $2,500,000 to the Metropolitan Museum from the estates of John Hoge, of Zanesville, Ohio, and J. B. Dick and Isaac Fletcher, both of New York City. Also there are listed the bequest to the city of Philadelphia of the J. G. Johnson collection of paintings, valued at over $3,000,000; the bequest of the painter Henry W. Ranger, to the National Academy of

Design, of about $200,000, the income to be used to purchase paintings by contemporary American artists; the gift to the Minneapolis Society of Fine Arts, from an anonymous donor, of the William Ladd collection of etchings, valued at $225,000; and, from Mrs. Mary Warden Harkness, a bequest of $100,000 to the Cleveland Museum, and the promise of her collection, to go to the museum at a later date.

Notable among the recent benefactions to the profession directly was the establishment at Oyster Bay, Long Island, of

THE TOLEDO MUSEUM OF ART

the Louis Comfort Tiffany Foundation. This is the gift by Mr. Tiffany of his home, his art collections, and a large endowment fund for the establishment of a school or colony of growing artists. The purpose is to provide an atmosphere in which serious young artists who have received the usual academic instruction and have given evidence of real creative ability may find themselves amid stimulating and sympathetic surroundings. Fortunately no distinction is made in favor of the so-called "fine arts," and workers in the "industrial arts" will be admitted on the same footing.

The Federal government offers one major instance of interest, as a balance for this continuous course of development in popular support. Congress, in response to a very noble plan presented by men like McKim, the architect, in the nineties provided for the American Academy in Rome, where the best of our native talent could be brought in contact with the splendid heritage of classic culture. Since its inception this institution has flourished and become greatly enlarged in scope.

It is not likely that the patronage of the government will ever be more than casual, and indeed a casual interest is preferable in the opinion of many artists, who are apprehensive of losing their freedom under the growth of an official patronage. Nevertheless, a movement is under way to induce the government to create a Secretaryship of Public Education, as a first step toward the establishment of a national office of Commissioner of Fine Arts.

The museum director, owing to his responsibility in the educational program, is beginning to be recognized in this country as a member of a special and important profession, as he has long been recognized abroad. There men with a thorough academic training, and a special knowledge of archæology and also of the equally broad field of modern art, are put in charge of the museums. In the past we have sometimes made use of artists, with executive ability and possessed of a broad culture, as curators of our museums and galleries, and in many such instances we have done conspicuously well. At other times the professional publicity man has fitted in, welding a bond between the public and his institution by providing information and sometimes instruction. Eventually we shall take art administration as a profession, as definitely as engineering or law.

As a result of increasing recognition the artist, individually, now enjoys better advantages than heretofore, although he has no specific or defined guarantees to rely upon. There are now approximately five thousand professional artists in the United States, the numbers decreasing as one travels westward. Their influence, as collectively expressed in societies and other organizations, is making itself felt for the good of the commonwealth. The public, on the whole, hesitates to patronize the artist directly, preferring to obtain whatever art product it desires through the agency of dealers. The lack of accessible and inviting quarters for artists in many cities, outside of the big centers, is often the cause of this condition. Many of our art dealers show little interest in American art. There is obviously not the same profit in dealing in American works of art, since the standard of living at home does not permit the American artist to compete in price with his European colleague,—particularly now, with the decline in value of European currency. It is obviously much more profitable for our dealers to buy pictures and other works of art in Europe. With the exception of a few genuinely interested men who had faith and the courage of their convictions, American art dealers in the past have been of little help to the American artist.

Therefore the one agency to which the artist here in America must look is the direct patronage of the public, the practical support of that part of the community which is discriminating and sympathetic. It is often only a small group, but wherever it exists it is the mainstay of artistic existence. No reliable statistical material regarding the total amount of money expended on art in the United States is available, but the sum is unquestionably very generous. The great industrial prosperity of this country causes wealth increasingly to be applied to the promotion of the arts. America is, for the capable, original artist, as desirable a country to live in as it was discouraging only fifty years ago. America is beginning to be recognized as genuinely interested in art; and since the conditions abroad will for many/years not be conducive to a liberal patronage of the fine arts, many European artists are looking toward America for a market. Twenty years ago this would have been a detriment to American artists, for we should easily have yielded to the fascination of a foreign subject and name; but the American artist is beginning to be so firmly established in the affection of his own people that national pride alone will safeguard him against foreign competition. Times have changed: though we have yet to give, on a large scale, a representative American art exhibition abroad, the feeling prevails there, nevertheless, that we are in a fair way successfully to assert our own artistic ideals alongside of the art of the Old World. It is still customary for the European to attribute the success of many of our leading artists to European training, but the number of those who are rooted in home influence is becoming larger every year.

The recent decline of European civilization and the economic breakdown of the Old World have made it possible for us to acquire works of art which, previous to the war, were not obtainable at any price. There are some instances on record where, long before the World War, Americans at public auctions set new records in paying extraordinary prices for well-known foreign works of art. Mr. William H. Crocker, of San Francisco, was able to purchase in the early nineties, for a very large amount, "The Man with the Hoe," by Millet; and very recently the purchase by Mr. Huntington, of Pasadena, of Gainsborough's masterpiece "The Blue Boy," for his excellent collection of British full-length portraits, has been widely commented upon. The change in the fortunes of the European aristocracy will, undoubtedly, make available a great many masterpieces for the American collector. The effect of this will be reflected in an increased national pride and a continuous demand for better standards in art. Every indication points toward the development of our country as a center of art.

XVIII

THE PLACE OF ART IN EDUCATION

The value of art as an educational factor of far-reaching importance was recognized by the ancient Greeks, and in modern education, once more, its potency for good through very many channels is being emphasized. It is only in recent years, however, that we have fully recognized this desirability of art in American education. The high value of art is demonstrated beyond doubt, since it is admitted that all art, aside from being a means of expression, is a striving for perfection. The emotional element in art also makes it an effective means in shaping and controlling the behavior of the individual and of society. This the Greeks undoubtedly knew, and they made full use of it. It is beginning to be understood more clearly that the solution of important social problems is furthered by providing through the medium of art a release for the pent-up emotions of our people. There is no more convincing evidence of this than to look back into the history of our communities and see what life meant in the days when art galleries, symphony orchestras, and the drama were either entirely lacking or available only to a small, restricted group. American life is assuming meaning, color, and values through the instrumentality of art. Its highest ideals will never mature unless we fully appreciate that fact and develop a means for the teaching of art in our scheme of education. Although we may all *believe* in art, the practical demonstration of some method of training which will give the high-school and college student an understanding of the meaning of art has not been achieved. Although no enlightened educator questions the desirability of art as an important agency of cultural education, educators are not yet convinced that a method has been developed for teaching an understanding, an appreciation, of art so that this potential power of art may, in a systematic way, be set to work among all students. There is, no doubt, a good deal of rhapsodizing about art everywhere, even among teachers, and methods of teaching art are neither uniform nor definite. Too often the art teacher in the high schools is the product of special technical training without a general cultural background in art; in fact, he often holds a special vocational certificate as the authority for his right to teach. His training at present is largely along technical lines; and whenever theory has been studied, it is likely to be the theory of design or color, which he investigates largely with a view to improving his own ability to produce works of art, rather than to incorporating the various principles of formal beauty into a method of teaching the appreciation of art. The requirements for the training of art teachers stress too greatly the technical factors; and unless we greatly modify our teachers' training requirements by balancing technical practice with cultural discipline, our art teachers will continue to be in a special technical class.

More attention should be devoted to æsthetics, art history, and the development of a faculty for the practical discrimination of what constitutes the difference between good art and bad. If æsthetics is a branch of philosophy, and philosophy is capable of methodical processes, there is no reason why our art teachers should be content with the demonstration of technical skill. This has its unquestioned value, but, after all, only to a limited number of students in technical courses. The problem is emphasized in the training of art teachers in many colleges and schools. The experience of the University of California may be taken as a typical illustration of the general confusion in the system of art education, in which candidates for teaching are referred to at one time as teachers of art and at another as teachers of drawing. We would not ordinarily refer to an instructor in English as a teacher of penmanship; yet the distinction between the technical field of drawing and the general field of art is just as great.

Only fifteen years ago the California State Board of Education certified graduates of the colleges of letters and sciences of the State University as teachers of art, on the showing that they had satisfactorily passed a six months' course in drawing in charcoal from plaster casts. Since then great changes have come about, due to a number of factors. At present the requirements for a prospective teacher of art, at the University of California, include a variety of technical courses, such as scientific perspective, design, drawing and painting, artistic anatomy; but they demand also that one third of the total requirement be in art history and the philosophy of the beautiful, divisions of the general study of æsthetics in the department of philosophy. It will be readily seen that a technically equipped teacher who has been trained in the history of human achievement in the field of art, and who has also been thoroughly grounded in the scientific facts, will make a type of instructor who, though perhaps only a fairly good performer, will be a much better teacher than one lacking a broad background. The art teacher will then not fail in demonstrating what educators like Professor Judd[1] and others expect of him; however, this demonstration has yet to be made in many schools. Professor Judd's challenge, that the art teachers must demonstrate "that there is no fundamental opposition between the habits of mind and action cultivated in the arts and those cultivated in the scientific courses given in the schools," has yet to be answered. There exists a necessity for marked differentiation between technical instructors and teachers of the appreciation of art. Our American collegiate art departments, which are often charged with the training of art teachers, have still extraordinarily varying programs. Some college art departments give no technical instruction whatever; often this is offered only by the school of architecture. Again, the instruction is exclusively technical, and its relation to a general cultural program in the college of arts and sciences

[1] Charles Hubbard Judd, Psychology of High School Subjects, pp. 363, 364. Ginn and Company, 1915.

is limited. The æsthetician, the art historian, the archæologist, who constitute most necessary factors in the scheme of preparation of the art teacher, prefer to be identified with the departments of philosophy, history, or Latin. Consequently the art teachers in many colleges remain by themselves, as a sort of fifth wheel; but wherever they have definitely assumed larger cultural responsibilities, their efforts have been well received. The late Professor Dow, a leader in his day, and a man whose influence upon many art teachers is well recognized, devoted his energies to the promoting of design as the open sesame to a critical understanding of art. His attitude represented the reaction against the popular prejudice in favor of content in art. His belief in synthetic approach, through the study of design as opposed to unselective imitation, is shared by many. In questioning the value of "drawing" in the latter sense, he wrought beneficial changes among many art teachers who flocked to his standard. There can be no doubt that his influence has been far-reaching and in the right direction. But the teaching of design, however much it promotes the critical powers and develops judgment, does not produce art teachers capable of espousing and explaining through language either the principles of beauty or the history and appreciation of art. It is along these lines that art teaching in the high schools and also in higher institutions is capable of improvement.

A brief survey of the historic development will convince everyone that the methods and agencies which address themselves to the task of art teaching are as many as they are varied. The beginnings were meager enough; and after nearly a century of experimentation a clear definition of the respective responsibilities and aims is still lacking.

Since art is so deeply rooted in the feelings and the existence of man, it naturally entered into teaching very early, although not as a formally recognized subject. Art education in the United States may be said to have had its beginning simultaneously with the opening of the doors of the first school, or even with the particular log the two ends of which were occupied respectively by teacher and pupil.

We know, from educational records, of the introduction of drawing into the Girls' High School of Boston as far back as 1826, and into the English Classical School in 1829. The study of literature antedates the introduction of the mechanical arts by many years. Music appears as a special subject of study in the high school of Northampton, Massachusetts, in 1837; and it was a popular subject, particularly with girls. Gradually other subjects have been added, such as the arts of design, which at present are found in the curriculum of nearly every high school. Owing to the breakdown, in modern times, of the apprentice system in many of the practical arts, the high schools now have assumed the responsibility for training young people in the many mechanical and vocational arts. There is great doubt in the minds of those who have enjoyed the advantage of an apprenticeship under the old, somewhat paternal systems whether this innovation is really taking the place of the former system. In the meantime the growth in the teaching of art subjects has been gradual and consistent. At present many of the arts are given very generous attention in the secondary-school system of America, and, indeed, it is possible to recognize architecture, painting, sculpture, music, literature, the drama, and the dance, either under their true names or in some disguised form, on the programs of many of our up-to-date high schools. These subjects may be emphasized in their æsthetic aspect or in their practical aspect; more often the practical side predominates, to the exclusion of the æsthetic. With slight exceptions, æsthetic training in the high schools is not attempted save in connection with literature. The reason for this, as we have seen, is to be found in the lack of properly trained teachers.

Art education along æsthetic lines will hardly be possible, in schools of secondary grade, below the last year in high school. The immaturity of the student of grammar-school age makes an analytical study of æsthetic principles too difficult a task.

Literature, to a very considerable extent, lays in the high schools a foundation for the more thorough understanding of the other arts. It is in literature that order, composition, structure, form, and the philosophy of the beautiful are presented. This is particularly emphasized in the study of poetry, which depends more than prose upon purely abstract elements of art. In prose the content invariably makes the major appeal, rather than abstract form. It is here that much of the general predilection for content in art is developed; this prejudice is one of the greatest stumblingblocks in the way of the full appreciation of art.

However, if it is a fact that the creating of what we call art will always be restricted to a chosen few who are endowed generously by nature, an understanding of art values through educational means must be made as widespread as possible. Only thus will the layman be prepared to appreciate the work of the artist, and only thus will the artist eventually secure the moral support and patronage which result from an understanding of his aims and achievements.

The majority of people are endowed by nature with an instinctive feeling for æsthetic pleasures. This feeling is natural and must be supplemented, but the true appreciation of what constitutes the finest flower of art may be acquired only by mastery of the principles. To quote a Professor of Education: "With the fewest exceptions, real enjoyment of the arts must be prepared for by training, for the simple reason that their practice is not natural. The arts represent an artificial refinement, perfected by the ages, and their appreciation requires abilities less only in degree than the ability required for their creation. The very history of the arts outlining as it does their slow development through the ages from the crudest beginnings to highly developed forms is enough to indicate the truth of this contention. What it takes one man a lifetime to prepare for and to execute, another cannot enjoy offhand."[1]

[1] John Louis Horn, The American Elementary School, p. 323. The Century Co., 1923.

Though few people fail to comprehend and enjoy the intellectual significance of a work of art, they fail conspicuously in the effort to comprehend those reasons that cause competent critics to single out certain pictures or works of sculpture or architecture for enjoyment and high praise. It must therefore be evident that art education in our schools must emphasize to our young people the significance of form as well as content. Civic art as a special problem would not exist if the appreciation of formal beauty did not so lamentably lag behind the incessant emphasis on subject appeal.

An education in art perception is naturally more easily obtained where the conditions are favorable; that is, where original works of art may be studied in museums and galleries, and also where people feel and think and talk about art as a necessary part of their lives. But there are many possibilities for the study of art in almost all communities.

Our country in the past has perhaps not unjustly been accused of excessive materialism and of lack of real culture; but that accusation is no longer tenable today, and our schools are feeling the beneficial reactions of this change. We have now not only many technical courses in art as a part of our regular school system, but we have also numbers of flourishing art schools. Our system of professional art education originally was shaped after European patterns of the type devoted, in the main, to the so-called fine arts,—the academy, instead of schools for teaching the artistic expression of the practical, useful things needed most at the moment. We are acknowledging this early mistake in the eagerness with which we are now providing technical schools for teaching the value of art appeal in things actually needed. In a civilization of material development this practical relation of art to industry offers great opportunities. The movement is in many ways a good one.

At the beginning of the last century, such art schools as existed in this country were academies of the European type; at present the number of schools of applied art in existence is increasing so rapidly as to assume the right proportion.

This is the result of the awakening of a national understanding that the art of a people is a question of living in well-designed surroundings, in houses which demonstrate the application of artistic principles to every detail, or of orderly arranged and harmoniously formed interiors and exteriors which reflect an understanding of artistic principles. Foreign critics in the past have been justified in their observations that we spend money for pictures which we often put into houses lacking in every quality of art. The artistic principles found in the formal value of a good picture should be recognized and desired in all our surroundings; there are the same potential elements of formal beauty in a picture as in a piece of furniture.

Our art schools are now engaged in organizing their classes with regard to our needs. Unfortunately, soon after we set up housekeeping in America at the end of the eighteenth century, art in Europe had started on its period of decline, only here and there relieved by symptoms of revival of classic formulas. The interest in the useful arts was carried on only by the endless and meaningless imitations of Renaissance, Romanesque, or Gothic ornamentation; and in the case of the so-called higher arts there was for nearly a hundred years a preoccupation with anecdotalism and romanticism in general. Eventually, toward the end of the last century in Europe, the reaction set in, in the form of a renewed interest in original art based upon utilitarian needs. In Europe there arose at that time a desire to find new and heretofore neglected forms of ornamental decoration indigenous to the localities in which they were used. Picture-making, as the only art expression, suddenly lost its monopoly. In the nineties many very talented local painters abroad became conscious of the narrowness of their outlook and began to apply their talents to that large and fruitful field of applied art, the designing of useful things. We can only hope that a similar impulse may assert itself in talented younger art students of our day who are working, often against their own convictions, along the narrow traditional lines.

Similarly, as our universities have become American institutions, outgrowing the European institutions after which they were patterned, the desire for technical education has assumed such proportions as to overshadow the study of the classics. This, many are convinced, is merely a temporary symptom, which will remedy itself with the changing of our industrial civilization into one more cultural. We are, it is admitted, at present in a marked state of transition and experimentation.

In trying to determine the educational status of art, we cannot afford to ignore the modern university in America, where all studies—the classics, the humanities, the sciences, and finally the arts—exist side by side in a unified whole. Those who are acquainted with European institutions of similar name but of very different organization will readily perceive the advantages of having our young people attend American universities. In the European university there is no such centralization as in America; there is a definite restriction to the old-time "humanities." In Europe the technical colleges, such as mining and engineering, and the professional schools—law and medicine—are conducted in separate institutions governed by special requirements. The student in such an institution must stimulate his æsthetic sense outside of his studies. The possibilities and encouragement for undirected study in that direction are, of course, far greater in Europe than in America. In some universities in America the foundation for an understanding and appreciation of all the arts may now be secured. Such centralization may have its defects, particularly when one remembers that the American university as a type owes its existence to expediency rather than to plan. In the end, however, our universities, with their close association of many subjects, will result in a very generous culture,—not one-sided, but genuine in its recognition of all phases of human activities, including æsthetic expressions. It would be difficult to find a university abroad where a general student with a natural bent for art, in order to support and augment his technical studies leading to his life work, could take courses in classical archæology, the history of architecture and of art in general æsthetics, the appreciation of art, the theory of design and color,—to name the purely theoretical subjects alongside of many practical ones. The possibilities of this all-embracing curriculum offered by some of our universities are at once novel and effective, educating young people not only for the professions outside the so-called fine arts, but giving also, to a student of law, economics, medicine, engineering, agriculture, or chemistry, an opportunity to lay a foundation for an interest in the finer things of life that may ultimately become the saving grace and happiness of his later years. The breadth of such work and the possibility of enjoying its benefits under one roof constitute a most interesting aspect of the American university. Art in some of our universities and colleges, however, has not yet assumed its rightful importance. Unless we put all the so-called fine arts and music on the same basis of importance as literature in our colleges, we shall never be successful in our cultural aspirations. In some universities and colleges the inclusion of a few courses in free-hand drawing in the college curriculum is still regarded as a genuine recognition of art.

That the recognition of art as being on a par with other cultural subjects has not been achieved anywhere in the universities of the United States is undoubtedly to some extent also the result of the vocationalizing of the subject. It is very doubtful whether art training in the colleges—that is to say, in the colleges of letters and sciences—should be vocational. As much practice as makes for better appreciation should be given; but, in general, the purpose of art-teaching in college should be the same as that of the teaching of literature, history, or even science. To broaden and deepen the understanding and the sympathy and to permit intelligent usefulness should be the chief aim of art-teaching in the colleges. Professor Frank Jewett Mather, Jr., of Princeton, holds to the conviction in these words[1]: "It is a proper aim of college art

[1] "Art in the College," *The American Magazine of Art*, January, 1923.

instruction to make the connoisseur, the man whose vital responses to beauty have been scrupulously sorted, intellectualized, checked and compared, the magically alert eye and all-embracing taste."

A very important need in art education is to provide in all our schools and colleges for the study of the æsthetic traditions in art, stressing the fact that man has at all times endeavored to express ideas and objects in such a way as to give æsthetic pleasure. A general museum of art, dedicated to all the arts that may be visually enjoyed, with its broad educational activities, of which the Metropolitan Museum in New York and the Art Institute in Chicago are conspicuously successful examples, is the type of institution needed to help in this program. Under the supervision of the universities the art museums will be able to maintain the highest standards. The art museum governed by popular standards often is a storehouse of collected things which may be of interest from a sentimental and historical point of view; even this, perhaps, has some value in developing interest in art. The properly classified and catalogued museum of authenticated and evaluated things is possible, generally, only long after the first stage has laid a foundation for the understanding and interest of the next generation. The change from the first to the next will depend upon the growth of intelligent interest in the community and on the guidance of experts. We might well establish, at our museums under university control, schools for the training of museum directors, to care for the needs of a profession which at present recruits its members from many different sources.

The development of a special educational system may be observed in many of our art museums. The European museum, with its staff of government-appointed experts concerned largely with research, provides no educational program like that offered by our modern American museum. In Europe, with its deep-rooted class distinctions, art enjoyment on the whole is a privilege of the so-called upper classes. Membership in the privileged classes presupposes acquaintance with art, while other classes are not very seriously taken into account. With us it is now a common practice of those in charge of our American art institutes to supply in a democratic way the needs of many different social groups. Through the medium of lectures and special exhibitions at suitable times (even at night) special provision is made for children, and for the man in the street who finds it possible to come only on Sundays or at night. This policy of our art museums is most commendable and will undoubtedly in time bear good fruit. Visiting European experts have expressed surprise and approval of this educational function of our art institutions. The statement is widely attributed to some European leaders that in practical usefulness our American art museums are superior to similar institutions abroad, and many of our citizens feel that the compliment is well deserved.

The development of the larger understanding of art cannot be accomplished merely by providing for technical instruction. The college probably is not the place for elaborate or advanced technical training in any line, which should be left for the graduate schools or the technical schools. It is becoming more and more evident that before the professional schools have any claim, stress in the college should be laid on broad culture. In the colleges the foundation of taste should be laid, so that a graduate may have sound convictions on art. College courses in art, then (aside from teachers' training-courses), should be directed largely toward the development of taste—the appreciation, the intelligent enjoyment, of art. The college, then, is the place to study art as a part of human achievement in the past as well as in the present. This study of the theory and the history of art open up fundamental truths. Theory, history, and practice should assume normal relations in their common contribution to the formation of a student's convictions on the very large and important subject of art.

In order to remedy the present confusion in the field of art instruction, it is necessary first for those in authority to admit that the subject has two distinct aspects, which involve different approaches. The purely technical, mechanical aspect is very well taken care of, as the actual output of beautiful objects in our school exhibitions amply proves. There is no dearth of teachers in the vocational, technical field; in many colleges and high schools technical instruction is of a high order. But there is little or no supply of art teachers who are trained to teach art as a cultural subject. The scope of activity for this type is unlimited. The responsibility for the training of teachers of art in the broader sense rests with the agencies which train teachers.

We shall be able to enjoy our artistic efforts to the full only when we learn to understand art in whatever form it exists: as an emotional element in music, pictures, or poetry; as a formal element in wall papers, carpets, and illustrations, and also in the large and growing field of civic art.

Our native talents are so numerous and of such high order that they deserve the most enthusiastic support. Even with the present inadequate recognition, they have achieved great things. When we accord to our artists full understanding and sympathy, they will be able to give to the world a noble and enduring expression of our national ideals and those of the age.

INDEX

245

DATE DUE

DEC 22 1999	
MAY 0 8 2002	